Y0-CDN-878

THE KNOWLEDGE REVOLUTION

The Knowledge Revolution

Making the link between learning and work

Norman Evans

First published in 1981 by
Grant McIntyre Limited
39 Great Russell Street
London WC1B 3PH

British Library Cataloguing in Publication Data

Evans, Norman
    The knowledge revolution.
    1. Education, Higher
    I. Title
    378   LB2322

ISBN 0-86216-055-3
ISBN 0-86216-056-1 Pbk

Photoset in Great Britain by
Rowland Phototypesetting Limited
Bury St Edmunds, Suffolk
Printed and bound in Great Britain
at The Pitman Press, Bath

Contents

For
Winifred, Rachael, Richard, Harriet and Mark,
three generations
of
learners and teachers
with love

Acknowledgements

There are several groups of acknowledgements I want to make. In some ways they amount to a selective autobiography.

During the years when I was Director of Professional Studies and John Barnett was Principal of Culham College, Abingdon, and then when we were respectively Principals of Bishop Lonsdale College, Derby, and what is now the College of Ripon and York St. John, York, John Barnett and I were continually trying to devise ways of incorporating within degree courses periods of work or field experience as additional sources of learning to complement formal college study. The connection between those investigations and much of this book will be obvious to readers.

About eighteen months ago, Sir Charles Carter, Chairman of the Management and Research Committee of the Policy Studies Institute, and formerly Vice-Chancellor of Lancaster University, listened to some of the ideas offered in this book and since then has actively helped in finding ways to interest institutions of higher education in attempting developments within this field. Without that support I doubt whether this book would have been written. He read an early draft and made invaluable probing comments.

However, the most particular acknowledgement is of a fluke. A colleague fell sick, so in 1977 I accompanied a group of Bishop Lonsdale students to Keene State University in New

Hampshire as part of a student exchange that I had set up. Quite by chance, I noticed on someone's shelves a row of publications concerned with the assessment of experiential learning (learning acquired from work and life experience). I connected these with something else I came across by chance: an external degree based on individually-planned study programmes, originating in the knowledge a student had already acquired whatever its source – whether formal education, or work or life experience, it made no difference. That all linked with the ten-year discussion with John Barnett. This was my introduction to the work of CAEL (the Council for the Advancement of Experiential Learning).

From then on I have been very fortunate in learning at first hand of the developments in the United States from John Strange, who was Dean of the College of Public and Community Service (CPCS), University of Massachusetts, when I first knew him, and is now Vice-President of CAEL, and through him from Morris T. Keeton, President of CAEL; and also from Sheila Gordan, Dean of Co-operative Education in La Guardia Community College, New York; William Craft, Dean of the Open College, Bunker Hill Community College, Boston; Ruth Shane of Boston University; and Clarke Taylor of CPCS.

Over the last eighteen months the Kellogg Foundation has enabled me to visit many colleges and universities throughout the United States, for which I am deeply indebted, and through those visits I have learned much from countless members of faculty staff and students.

Especially in the early stages of these inquiries into American practices, little of the work could have been undertaken but for the hospitality of Jane and Steven Cohen, who gave me a home base on their side of the Atlantic, as well as great encouragement and support.

As well as an author, a book has an editor too, something often forgotten. Sarah Jane Evans of Grant McIntyre has been the very greatest help in ways both little and large, more than she probably knows.

Acknowledgements

With the very greatest pleasure and gratitude I acknowledge all the varied contributions to what has resulted as this book. Without them, its deficiencies would be greater.

Recently, I met a former student. He had wanted to switch from teacher training after his first year to a university to read English. After months of inconclusive correspondence, the college managed to persuade a somewhat reluctant university that he was perfectly capable of following their course. And so it proved. He is now doing a D.Phil. at Oxford. He symbolizes the hundreds of pupils and students in the schools and colleges where I have worked who have posed sharp questions about the relationship between their capacity for and interest in learning, and the institutions which, in name, exist to enable them to learn. So this book is an acknowledgement to all those young men and women who, without knowing it, have never let me forget for too long (I hope) that any education institution fails learners in as far as it fails to respond to them and expects them to do the responding: 'Tell me and I forget; teach me and I remember; involve me and I understand'. This acknowledgement to them becomes then a call for higher education to respond to learners so that potential students may more readily become involved.

Norman Evans

pared with spending it on health, housing and transport.

Each of these issues relates to the overriding political question concerning education: the distribution of political and economic power. So far, generally speaking, graduates have higher expectations of their personal and professional lives and of their general standing and influence than others. Who attends higher education and what they do afterwards are weighty political matters. By itself, education cannot solve these problems, but it could certainly be more active than at present in trying to help find solutions. What matters for taxpayers and householders is that there should be public evidence of education showing determination to tackle these problems and doing so because of their importance to ordinary people.

The focus of this book is higher education. Its theme is that higher education can convince members of the public that it is working on their behalf, provided that it changes its stance and is seen to be taking careful account of the conditions of ordinary people. It proposes that higher education is likely to find its most promising future through concentrating as its first priority on a systematic reconsideration of styles of academic learning and teaching. It needs to do this to take full account of a more heterogeneous student body than at present. The days when 18-year-old entrants predominated are over, with the increase in the number of older students. Demography and technology suggest that changes in student recruitment are bound to come. If higher education is to flourish and recruit sufficient students it will need to develop study facilities designed for the men and women who are the potential students of the late 1980s and 1990s. That means taking cues from their occupational, domestic and social circumstances. Evidence of making these matters top priority could do as much as anything to strengthen public support for education. For higher education the importance is ultimately this: securing the financial base for its essential contributions to research and all post-secondary education.

Almost certainly, then, seeking the most promising future

means being prepared to do things differently, whilst maintaining current academic standards. Vital questions on the organization of academic courses and their structure, as well as their content, need to be faced. It may well mean some institutions doing less of what they are doing at present in full-time three- or four-year courses in two or three disciplines, taught largely from 9 AM to 5 PM. It may mean undertaking to teach part-time courses at inconvenient times and in inconvenient places. It certainly means that any adjustments to present academic services have to be made within existing resources. Developments needing additional funds are not even worth talking about. Ingenuity, imagination and flair are going to be at a premium.

This could be presented as a very gloomy future, but it need not be so. Within a scheme of priorities which gives precedence to the circumstances of the widest range of potential students, research can still be sustained as the prime responsibility of higher education for extending the boundaries of knowledge through pure and applied studies. By paying careful attention to the largest number of students, all else can follow. Initiatives which provide the most effective styles of learning and teaching for the coming decades must include giving formal recognition to the knowledge and skills held by men and women irrespective of how they have acquired them or whether they have paper qualifications to prove it. No one disputes that each person is learning continually through informal means without reference to educational institutions. But the formal systems rarely take any account of this learning. The thesis here is that educational institutions should take official and public account of what people know and can do in the search for the best modes of learning and teaching. If there is evidence of learning attainments equivalent to those required for entry to higher education or at undergraduate or graduate levels it should be recognized as such. Further, such recognition has to be given without any weakening of present academic standards.

To do this demands a willingness to consider afresh what all categories of students wish to learn and how best they can be helped to learn, rather than beginning from the courses which are provided at present. It means academic staff accepting the full implication of the fact that institutions of higher education do not have a monopoly of their students' learning. It means building a clear relationship between the learning acquired through formal educational provision and all the other kinds of learning which take place. For many teachers in higher education it means substantially reconsidering their academic responsibilities, and accepting different roles. The case made here is that, through paying deliberate attention to all the learning which takes place right outside its responsibilities, teaching in higher education would become more effective (because more appropriate), and so more sought after. Systematic consideration of informally independently-acquired learning would be a catalyst for higher education's brighter future.

Before the days of compulsory schooling, for most people there was no sharp division between what they learned in one sphere or another. How much of an apprentice carpenter's steady acquisition of skills and knowledge came from his workplace and the instruction of his master craftsman, and how much from daily conversations, from casual observation, from his home, was not significant. What mattered was what the apprentice could achieve; that is what his master judged. In some ways, discussion about informally-acquired learning falls into the same mould. In a modern technological society, learning is going on all the time for vast numbers of people, as they live and work. What matters most is what they can acquire. It is the effective combination of the various kinds of learning which enables them to do most; that is what society needs from its members.

We live in a society in which the need for learning is more pronounced than ever. It is difficult to think of occupations which do not require employees to be learning almost continually. In industry, production processes change in rapid succession so that production workers, supervisors and managers are having to adapt, acquiring new skills and extending their understanding of the tasks they are expected to perform. In commerce, the collection, storage and retrieval of information increase in efficiency, sophistication and extent. This makes persistent demands on employees to master new techniques and use them in a comprehensive understanding of their particular function in the entire establishment. The majority of employees now, whatever the colour of their collars, find that they are required to be learners. In comparative terms these character-istics of our society can easily be exaggerated. The social and economic changes which followed the introduction and development of steam power and railways were every bit as dramatic. But there is one aspect of contemporary change which touches higher education directly. More people need to work effectively with words and numbers at a relatively more advanced level. It is the nineteenth century's story but at a higher education level. Then the development of schools was partly a response to the demand for larger numbers of literate employees. The expansion of higher education in the mid and late twentieth century has been in part to supply increasing numbers of graduates required by industry and commerce and especially the professions.

The homes we live in have always been places of learning. Now, however, the nature and range of that learning is different. So much of it is acquired in the first instance through words spoken, and seen, as well as read. By law, most of the items which are bought for daily use at home, whether food or equipment, are labelled with significant technical information about the product. As consumers, we are being exhorted to read the information carefully and become more discriminating. Advertisements which appear in the newspaper, on the tele-vision, through the letter box and in the shop similarly invite us to consider the virtues of products according to the detailed specification provided. The entire span of statutory obligations and entitlements which affect each household, from income tax and rates and rent regulations through to schooling and social services, poses another set of learning requirements. The press and media provide an unceasing flow of information, much of which is assimilated and learned. Holidays are increasingly offered as occasions which can be deliberately used for learning, through study travel tours at home and abroad, formal classes in a holiday setting, or traditional summer schools. The do-it-yourself movement has spread through every imaginable activity from house building and gardening to international radio monitoring, wool dyeing, and spinning and weaving. The boom in cookery book sales tells its own story. So does the number of people who travel to museums and places of scenic and historical interest. We are not only being offered information for learning, but we are positively seeking out more of it in every conceivable sphere.

So a considerable amount of active, purposeful and deliberate learning is now a characteristic of a very large proportion of the individual members of our society, and much of this learning is anything but trivial. It becomes the basis for action; whether at work or at home or at leisure, we have to go on learning simply to be able to deal with a never-ending series of decisions. Every technological society faces the same development: the learning society.

In such a society it is obvious that higher education will develop. The critical issues are the kinds of growth which are most in the interests of the individuals making up that society. The inner significance is the health and well-being of higher education itself; it needs to be confident in what it is doing. In the present circumstances this is extraordinarily difficult. The problems seem endless. At present the system is driven by the need to sustain student enrollments and confused by conflicting predictions. Necessarily, seeking to attract different kinds of students raises anxieties about endangering academic standards. A relatively static system resulting from financial restrictions implies a larger annual salary bill as academic staff get older. An ageing staff within a static system conjures the dreadful spectre of a missing generation of scholars, as appointments for young men and women become even scarcer. The tendency of students' employers and some government ministers to view higher education as a narrow rather than a broad vocational preparation raises fundamental questions about the curriculum, questions which also affect the relationships between higher education and the schools, sixth-form colleges and colleges of further education where the 16 to 19 year olds are taught. Accountability for finance and provision are acknowledged as serious issues, but hardly acknowledged at all there remains accountability of purpose. Attempts at planning to provide a coherent set of answers raise complex issues about institutional administration and local and central government. It is small wonder that heads of institutions are in constant danger of being grossly overloaded, thus raising searching questions about the quality of institutional leadership.

Even so, higher education's health and well-being is governed primarily by the nature of the relationship between its provision of courses and the numbers of students studying them. Whatever the significance of research programmes for essential academic development, and whatever their quantity, it is the total number of institutions engaged in teaching first degrees and the total number of students being taught for them which establish the crude framework within which higher education as a whole is considered. Unless the numbers of students are adequate to justify the continuance of the present number of institutions providing courses, some are under threat of contraction, and others of closure. The other way of expressing that issue is to say that the courses themselves need considering, along with the ways of studying them, in terms of their attractiveness to potential students. Either way, morale is the vital factor. Threats of closure may sharpen perceptions; by themselves they are unlikely to improve the services offered.

It is a relatively new experience for higher education to be discussed in terms of an anxiety for too few students (and the sooner that negative approach can be replaced by a more positive sense of purpose the better for everyone concerned). Until comparatively recently the anxiety was for the opposite reason: not enough places for the large number of applicants seeking entry. Some discussions of the reasons for this change come later; here it is sufficient to establish the point. Predictions of student numbers have been successively reduced. Through the UGC the Government is now simply reducing numbers by fiat.

In Britain the Robbins Report[1] published in 1963, set in train the most dramatic expansion of higher education this country had yet seen. In 1962 there were 216,000 full-time higher education students. It predicted that there would be 558,000 students in 1980/81. In 1970 Education Planning Paper No 2 published by the Department of Education and Science (DES) forecast 835,000 full-time students in 1981/82. That was the highest peak of expectation, for the White Paper Cmnd 5174 published in 1972 gave 750,000 as the number for 1981. Two years later, the Public Expenditure White Paper for 1974/75 (Cmnd 5879) gave a figure of 640,000 for 1981/82, which was further reduced in the Public Expenditure White Paper for 1975/76 (Cmnd 6393) to 600,000 for 1981/82. Since then there have been sundry other predictions, none of which is likely to prove any more reliable. There was a whisper that, within the DES, 560,000 was the assumption for 1981, and that the figure for 1979 was about 530,000. This becomes more important because the demographic evidence shows that within the present pattern of provision, entry and study, the numbers of 18 year olds drops so markedly from the mid 1980s to the mid 1990s that the figure predicted for the 1990s is 450,000. While that may be just as unreliable as previous attempts at predicting student numbers, it has to be taken as a clear sign that for higher education things have changed. New categories of students have to be found.

Numbers of students is the crux of the matter for higher education. But deductions from demography, and obsessions with attempting to devise more sophisticated ways of predicting

[1] 'Higher Education', Cmnd 2154, HMSO.

numbers, seems essentially a passive, even negative, way of considering the future for higher education. Its future lies within the learning society. There is evidence that plenty of people not only enjoy learning, but that many more are seeking it, and increasing numbers are going to need it as an integral part of their employment. The essential debate then, which can be conducted with a positive intent to remove the anxiety about the future, concerns the relationship between the institutions which offer higher education and the individual members of the learning society. It has to be conducted on the understanding that at best higher education will have no more resources than it has at present. So the debate concerns possible developments facilitated by redeploying existing resources, which means less higher education of the kind we have, and more of kinds we have little of at present, and perhaps some entirely new kinds altogether. It means a wider range of provision, perhaps even of curricula to fit the circumstances of potential students.

This book examines what that could mean in practice. It begins with a consideration of the expansion of numbers in higher education following the Robbins Report and the establishment of polytechnics, and goes on to consider the consequences of the substantial disregard of some of the recommendations on the curriculum. The case is made that this disregard is in part responsible for the mismatch between what higher education is currently offering and the conditions and needs of large sections of the population. Although the needs of individuals are the starting point for this exploration of how education can serve them better, considerable attention has to be paid to the issues posed by any suggestion for change to the institutions and the staff who teach in them. The only point of any changes, however – and this is part of this book's theme – is to enable institutions to respond much more readily to individuals in their own particular circumstances; and the reader must not forget this. The first part of *The Knowledge Revolution* is a commentary on the failure so far to achieve this. This is followed by a chapter on some contemporary practices in

American higher education which indicate how matching can be achieved quite successfully between potential students and universities and colleges in a modern technological society. Many of these practices are useful pointers to the kinds of developments which can be attempted in Britain, and the next two chapters explore ways of trying to achieve the same kind of matching in this country. This is done from the point of view first of the potential students, and then of the academic staff and institutions. The concluding chapter sets out the case for a systematic extension of higher education facilities and a radical revision of the policies on which they are based.

2

The Years of Expansion

In 1963, what is now the much quoted Robbins formula rang out in Britain proclaiming an appropriate relationship between higher education and the individual members of society: '. . . That courses of higher education should be available to all who are qualified by ability and attainment to pursue them and who wish to do so'. It was convincing to those who knew that there were more able young people wanting to study than higher education places for them. Now it seems quite obvious. Then a Committee of Inquiry appointed by the Prime Minister was commissioned to 'review the pattern of full-time higher education in Great Britain and, in the light of national needs and resources, to advise Her Majesty's Government on what principles its long-term development should be based . . .' (*Robbins Report*, p. 1). Its Report established new principles.

As a basis for action the recommendation was that, within twenty years, the numbers in higher education should be more than doubled – 216,000 when the Report was being written and some 558,000 by 1980/81. But numbers alone was only one of the issues which the Robbins Report considered. The Committee went to some trouble to discuss the kinds of courses which would be appropriate for such expanded provision. They surveyed the courses then being offered by universities – there were no polytechnics or colleges customarily offering degree courses, save the Colleges of Advanced Technology which had been created as a result of the White Paper on Technical Education in 1957, and which conducted their academic work through the Council for Technological Awards. In paragraph 262, talking of 'broader degrees', the Report said, 'The present distribution of students between different types of honours course is unsatisfactory. A higher proportion should be receiving a broader education for their first degrees. This in itself calls for a change.' That applied to the 216,000 who were attending higher education in 1963. For the future, the Report went on, 'But if greatly increased numbers of undergraduates are to come into the universities in the future, change becomes essential. Indeed we regard such a change as a necessary condition for any large expansion of universities. Greatly increased numbers will create the opportunity to develop broader courses on a new and exciting scale, and we recommend that universities should make such developments one of their primary aims.'

In paragraph 138, in a discussion of the pool of ability and suitability for higher education, these words appear, talking of those who are between the very able and the very limited: 'But in between there is a vast mass whose performance, both at the entry to higher education and beyond, depends greatly on how they have lived and been taught beforehand.'

The combination of these assertions amounts to firm grounds for claiming that the Robbins Committee was making a serious attempt to identify ways in which an appropriate relationship between higher education and individuals could be developed. It is impossible to speak of broadly based courses, and of a role for higher education in training for the various skills which seemed to be required in 1963, and of acknowledging the significance of home and school experiences for a greatly increased number of students, without taking discussion of expansion far beyond the need for more higher education places. If these were the principles on which the Robbins Committee envisaged the dramatic expansion they were recommending, the story of the expansion has been somewhat different. Numerically the tale is quickly rehearsed.

When the Robbins Committee began its work, there were

118,000 students in universities, 55,000 students in teacher training colleges and 43,000 studying as full-time students on advanced courses in further education colleges (Table 3, p. 15). By 1975/76 there were 228,000 students on full-time and sandwich courses in universities, but the numbers in polytechnics and colleges had grown to 216,000 in all. The figures for 1978/79 stood at 285,000 for the universities, and 227,000 for polytechnics and other colleges. So in the sixteen years since the publication of the Robbins Report, the number of students on full-time study, technically known as advanced courses (including sandwich courses) has risen from 296,000 to 512,000. By any assessment that is a remarkable development.

The provision of courses is where the differences begin to show up between Robbins's views and what has happened. In any of the forty-five universities which now exist as chartered institutions after the Robbins Committee completed its work, there are many courses offered which might be described as broader in Robbins terms. Sometimes this breadth has been achieved by developing the kinds of combined honours courses which Robbins specifically mentioned. Sometimes it has been achieved through organizing the academic work of universities in Schools rather than Departments for the differing disciplines in a related field. There are not now many combinations of subjects which cannot be studied in one university or another. So in one sense something of the Robbins expectations, if not conditions, have been realized. When it comes to looking for courses which fall into the category of the skills Robbins referred to things are fairly clear. There has been considerable expansion of degrees with a professional preparation incorporated in them – accountancy, architecture, management, business studies (often with a foreign language included), nursing, not to mention the entire range of technological studies which have emerged from the universities which were created from the former Colleges of Advanced Technology. But when the search is for indications that the 'vast mass whose performance, both at entry and higher education and beyond, depends greatly on how they have lived and been taught beforehand' was in the forefront of the minds of the course designers, matters are anything but clear. Partly that is because there is no particular reason why the description of courses should offer that kind of evidence. Partly it is because there is no means of knowing except through direct experience how far the teaching of a course takes into account the way students have been taught beforehand.

What students sometimes have to say about the way they are taught, the most direct evidence there can be, does not suggest these considerations feature much in the minds of academic teachers, except negatively in complaints that their students are inadequately equipped to cope with the studies they have chosen. It is worth noting in passing that Robbins was well aware of the dangers of diminished standards through over-expansion; but had this to say of expansion '. . . and we must repeat therefore that they [increased numbers] make no allowance for any relaxation in the standards required to gain places.' And of those standards themselves, 'The present standards both in Universities and Training Colleges are, by common consent, considerably higher than the standards of the thirties and are almost certainly higher than those of the early fifties. In the thirties many students entered with qualifications below the present minimum: in the early fifties the minimum qualifications were generally the same as at present, but a higher proportion of those who possessed them were admitted. Yet it would be difficult to contend that the number receiving higher education in those decades contained an undue proportion of students incapable of substantial benefit from the process' (p. 169).

Robbins was a report about universities. From 1966, the polytechnics became major providers of higher education, for by 1972 all thirty designations had been made. They have contributed very considerably to the expansion of higher education as a whole. From 1972 onwards there have been the colleges and institutes of higher education created from the reorganization of teacher education,[1] and they too are now providing degree courses mainly of a general kind. Taking them all together, there were in 1979/80 536,000 students following first degrees, both full-time and sandwich courses. Once again, the story is quite straightforward numerically. The story of the courses ought to be different but in fact it is also similar. With all the emphasis on applied courses rather than the conventional academic ones that heralded the inception of polytechnics, it could have been expected that there would be rather more offered that was nearer to the Robbins conception; broader courses, designed in full recognition of the circumstances of the students. In fact the overlap of provision between polytechnics and universities is almost complete, save for one or two highly specialized and expensive courses such as medicine. The same is true, though perhaps more surprisingly, for the colleges and institutes of higher education. What has happened is that the expansion has been essentially more of what there was before, with some significant trimmings in some places, but nothing which approximates to the more radical implications of the Robbins Report.[2]

The expansion of higher education from 1963 was characterized by three- or four-year courses of full-time study, as residential as facilities would permit, and after 1968 (with the implementation of the Latey Report which removed the *in loco parentis* responsibility from institutions) generally for as long as students required, where study was concentrated on two or perhaps three subjects for an honours degree. Particularly in polytechnics, the number of sandwich courses[3] has increased, offering alternating periods of formal study and practical experience in engineering, or business management, accoun-

[1] David Hencke, *Colleges in Crisis*, Harmondsworth: Penguin, 1978.

[2] For a discussion of these issues as seen in 1970, see *Patterns and Policies in Higher Education* by George Buzzan, Charles Carter, Richard Layard, Peter Venables and Gareth Williams, Harmondsworth: Penguin Education Special, 1971.

[3] See Chapter 4; many co-op education courses offered in American institutions are shown to be similar to sandwich courses.

tancy, social administration, or the appropriate profession. Part-time degree study has increased largely through polytechnics, but again not sufficiently to make it a characteristic of higher education.

All this expansion has been built on the basis of the Robbins entry requirements: passes in at least five subjects in the General Certificate of Education, with at least two at Advanced Level. Entry to the first year of degree courses validated by CNAA often includes about fifteen per cent or more in a few cases without those formal qualifications, but usually those who are accepted have broadly similar qualifications to those admitted to universities through their various special admission procedures: the candidate tends to possess some formal professional qualification which is accepted as equivalent to two 'A' levels. The courses offered are still taught along the same lines; lectures, seminars, and in some institutions tutorials, all supported by the range of audio-visual aids according to the taste of the tutor. Laboratory work is the basis for science and technological studies.

Higher education in England and Wales is unique in having such a very low withdrawal rate (and such relatively short degree courses – mainly three years). It has rarely varied much from the fourteen per cent figure quoted in Robbins for universities.[1] For the rate to remain so very low is strong evidence of the attractiveness of the courses provided for those who undertake them. And the number of students who have kept coming forward as candidates has remained reasonably as expected, up until the last few years. (It is tempting but dangerous to compare withdrawal and completion rates in one country with those of other countries. There are so many variations in the duration of courses, in the length of time students take: to follow courses, to withdraw and then subsequently to enroll again, and in the reasons for registering at all, that any figures need many qualifications and ex-

[1] Op. cit., p. 52.

planations if they are not to be misleading. Then a table of comparisons becomes pointless.)

So the post-Robbins expansion has provided places for those who were both qualified for this level of study and who wished to follow a course. Or so it would seem. The missing piece is a comprehensive understanding of those 'who wish to do so', as Robbins put it. This is where some[1] take issue with what they claim was the Robbins conception of the future; that all that was required was more of what there was. Given the characteristics of the subsequent development that would appear fair comment. But to some extent critics leave out of account the views which were then expressed in the Report about the need for courses designed to foster the skills needed in our society, and take account of the circumstances of many of the additional students. It is not just to blame the Robbins Committee for developments which appear to have taken little account of those views; the institutions themselves must accept the responsibility. If on reflection they do appear to have taken inadequate account of some of the other parts of the Report, that in part is the reason for the discussion about the future of higher education becoming rather suddenly an urgent matter. Had the principle been followed of acknowledging the significance of home background and school experience, higher education would be more in touch today with the population. And it is important to remember Robbins was concerned with full-time higher education.

The most immediate reason for the urgency is that the numbers of students will decline, exacerbating the problems of finance. The demographic reasons for the likely decline are now well known. As the Permanent Secretary to the DES in January 1977 said, 'There are [in Great Britain] at the present time about 800,000 eighteen year olds. By the early 1980s this age group will have increased to a peak of well over 900,000; by the early 1990s it will have fallen to about 660,000 and will still be

[1] Eric Robinson, *The New Polytechnics*, Harmondsworth: Penguin, 1968.

falling. This clearly poses an excruciatingly difficult exercise in planning.'[1]

However, it is only part of the problem. Another important factor is the number of those who now 'wish to' study for degrees. All the signs are that these numbers are likely to decline quite sharply. The age participation rate (the number of eighteen year olds following higher education), as it is somewhat inelegantly called, was six per cent in 1961/62 according to the findings of the Robbins Committee. By 1972/72 it had risen to 14.2 per cent. It then fell to 13.4 per cent in 1975/76. Now, far from the confidence with which 15 per cent was used as a basis for the discussion of numbers by the DES in its discussion document *Higher Education in the 1990s*, some think that 13.5 per cent is the best to be hoped for, while gloomier informed but unofficial estimates can put the figure as low as 11 per cent. Whatever the reality, it is clear that there is no possibility of an increased participation by eighteen year olds compensating for the absolute reduction of numbers of young people alive at the time.

The significance of those 'who wish to do so' becomes compellingly obvious. Over the last twenty-five years, 'they' were more or less limited to those who possessed the formal qualification of the GCE or its equivalent. We have no means of knowing whether that limitation has meant that some of those who have wished to never got as far as considering themselves as candidates because the qualification hurdle looked much too high. What we do know is that despite the acknowledged need to increase the opportunities for the children of homes from all social classes, at the higher education level, just as the 1944 Education Act was intended to increase opportunities for school-aged children, the pattern of recruitment has remained more or less as it was in 1963. It is heavily weighted towards social classes I and II with a relatively tiny number coming from the homes of manual and semi-skilled workers.

[1] Speech to the Society of Education Officers, 27 January 1977.

The Final Report of the Conference of University Administrators published in 1978,[1] compiled by the Group on Forecasting and University Expansion, provides an admirable summary of the evidence available on what it describes as 'the most intractable of social problems'. That report gives the results of research into the social class of university students by percentages from 1955 to 1975. The figures show that consistently, within a point or two, the proportion of students from social classes I and II has remained at around 62 per cent. There has been some increase (about 4 per cent) in the representation of children from homes in the IIIN classification from 1961. But, correspondingly there has been an actual decline in the numbers coming from the manual classes III, IV and V, since 1944, from 25 per cent to 23 per cent. There is a tendency for social class IV and V to become smaller but nevertheless the Report says, 'We have no explanation for these figures. It does not seem likely that they can have been caused entirely by upward social drift. We can only speculate that the decline might represent in part a turning away from higher education by children whose parents fall into these classes.' This has coincided with government decisions to reduce expenditure on higher education – so that, either by accident, or by design, it looks as if numbers will be reduced anyway, through lack of money.

The Group also collated data concerning students in polytechnics. Although strict comparisons are not possible because of the categories and the timing of the information collected, the Report has this to say: 'Nevertheless, the two sets of data [Universities and Polytechnics] strongly suggest that the general class profile of degree students in universities is very similar, with the polytechnics drawing a rather smaller proportion of their entry from Social Classes I and II and rather more from III, IV and V.'

[1] Available through the Financial Secretary, The Registry, University of East Anglia, Norwich.

The Knowledge Revolution

This is no more than a reflection of what is happening in secondary schools, and has been happening ever since the introduction of secondary education for all under the 1944 Education Act. The succession of government reports on the subject serves to establish that. From *Early Leaving* (1953), covering the period from 1946, and the Crowther Report (1959) to the DES *Report on Education No 86*, which reported the results of a commissioned survey of 16 to 18 year olds in 1976, all tell the same tale. While there has been some increase in the number of children staying at schools for longer periods, proportionately the increase has been slower and slighter for the children from manual-class homes than for the others.

The latest confirmation of these trends comes from *Origins and Destinations: Family, Class and Education in Modern Britain*, a major research study by A. H. Halsey, A. F. Heath and J. M. Ridge published in 1980.[1] Their research shows that in 1972 1.8 per cent of the children from the homes of skilled and semi-skilled and unskilled workers in industry and agriculture, which made up 54.9 per cent of the entire population, entered universities. But some 20 per cent of the children from the homes of professionals, administrators and managers went to university, although these homes made up no more than 13.7 per cent of the population. Of the entrance qualification the authors feel able to say: '. . . Wastage of talent continues and was massive over most of the period with which we are concerned [birth cohorts 1913–52]' and 'By the seventies at least 7000 boys each year could have obtained A level passes but were not in fact remaining long enough at school to do so. Early decades showed numbers running at about 30,000 in the sixties, and 40,000 in the fifties.' They conclude that the number of working class boys qualifying for University entrance 'could be comfortably doubled without any necessary lowering of standards'. For girls the figures would probably be even more striking.

All this is borne out by accounts which can be given by the

[1] Oxford: OUP.

staff of schools and further education colleges attended by these potential students studying for their 'A' Levels, and by the admission tutors of colleges and universities.

Often some of the most promising students turn away from higher education because it seems quite remote from their familiar world. Almost any sixth-form tutor or careers adviser can produce innumerable stories of young men and women who are not able to jump the gap between their home environment, where there may well be little or no direct experience of what higher education means for individuals, and a college, polytechnic or university. The risks are seen as too great.[1] Until fairly recently there was a choice between taking a job and getting started as an earning adult, and a course of three or four years on a student maintenance grant. There was the risk of getting detached from home and locality and not being attached to anything in its place. There is now the further risk, as they see it, of not finding a satisfactory job at the end of the course. There is a very large concern for those who are uncertain about the course of study they might wish to follow. Many fear that, once started on a particular course, in most cases it is not at all easy to switch to another one if the first choice proves unsatisfactory. It is no good trying to counter these views by arguments which can prove they are hearsay, rather than reliable fact. To cite evidence from reports of the Central Service Unit for University and Polytechnic Careers and Appointments may have little effect although these show that employers are looking for more graduates than they can find, and that all the signs are that in this increasingly technological age, there will be a premium for employment on those with some form of higher education. So unhappily in part the expansion of higher education has provided opportunities which could not be used by large sections of the population for whom these additional places were intended. It is a familiar finding that facilities provided for all sections of the population are used more extensively by those who may

[1] Willy Russell, *Educating Rita*, Act 1 sc. II, Samuel French, 1981.

need them least. In higher education, the expansion of provision has not been sufficiently imaginative to convince large numbers of eighteen year olds that the greater opportunities for study were really intended for them.

Today this presents an important problem. In the relatively affluent past there were numbers of eligible eighteen year olds who were not convinced that higher education had anything to offer them. Now in a relatively difficult economic period the tendency will be for more to be sceptical at the stage when they choose between more formal education and beginning a job and a career with a steady income. Unemployment could have the opposite effect, of course. Eighteen year olds unable to find jobs could apply to higher education. For 1981/82 this appears to be the case in the United States. Applications are sixteen per cent up in public institutions and seven per cent up in private ones, according to a survey conducted for *The Chronicle of Higher Education* by John Minter Accountants,[1] despite a reduction in the number of eighteen year olds of 3.4 per cent in 1979. In Britain the problem does not seem so clear. But the key point here is that it is highly likely that a deferred entry pattern may evolve, as further qualifications are linked more specifically to promotion prospects. Some of those who were eligible and chose employment rather than further study at eighteen, could well be finding later that it is in their interests to have a degree. Would they then feel able to turn to higher education, would they then 'wish to do so' where their predecessors did not?

Other groups are already coming to the same position but along different routes; people who may not have wanted to use the opportunities that were available to them, but who now later in life begin to think they may wish to. Many men and women are finding either that they need to change their career in mid-life, or that they are required by their existing employer to undergo further training, simply because of the way so many industrial and commercial processes are developing. There are

[1] *Times Higher Education Supplement*, 13 March 1981.

many women who find when their children leave home, or need less attention, that they have a need to study, some for personal reasons, and some as a passport to employment. This is now a highly significant group both statistically and qualitatively. They may all have the requisite qualifications but have never needed to turn to higher education hitherto. As for the qualified 18-plus students who took jobs first and then changed their minds, falling into the deferred category of entry, the central question will be whether they now think that higher education offers them what they require at this stage of their personal development. All this is part of the attempt to have a better understanding of what those 'who wish to do so' really means for the rest of this century. A better understanding could lead to a more carefully thought-out relationship between individuals and institutions of higher education and that could be used as the basis for developing its provision.

Beyond these groups, however, may lie others equally important for higher education. These may also be those who were eligible for courses of degree study aged eighteen, and who are turning to those possibilities only later in life, perhaps somewhat to their surprise. These are the people who have reached their late forties or fifties and find themselves in what is somewhat euphemistically called early retirement. In other words they have been either dismissed or eased out of their jobs with some financial inducement, to make room for younger employees or to reduce the staff of their company. Some may well turn to courses of further study, partly in the hope of fitting themselves for some other occupation and partly for the sense of having something worthwhile to do. Some may be in the same category as those undergoing specific re-training, but if they are not sponsored by an employer the re-training purpose of the course will be extremely uncertain, making its usefulness all the more important. Usefulness is likely to appeal to another group: the retired who like the prospect of using some of their greater leisure time for study. These two groups could be of increasing importance for higher education.

It has been assumed that these groups fulfil the matriculation requirements on which the expansion of higher education was based. If the attempt to identify groups who now may 'wish to do so' goes beyond to groups who may not have formal qualifications, the search means asking different questions. These will be taken up in detail later, but in summary they can be posed in this way. Provided it can be shown that applicants without formal qualifications possess the knowledge and skills required for pursuing studies at degree level, there would appear to be no adequate reason for denying them the opportunity. If this was genuinely known to be possible, then every one of the groups mentioned so far could be increased very substantially.

Each of these groups could represent numbers of students who never came during the period of expansion, the very students for whom the expansion was intended. They may also represent numbers of students which the institutions will have need of if they are to fill their places. This is where demography and human interests intersect for a society which claims to be organizing its educational provision on the basis of equal opportunities. This is where the vision of the Robbins Committee shows its real significance, '. . . that the system will be judged deficient, unless it provided adequately for all'. In its turn that depends on a definition of 'qualification, by ability and attainment to pursue them [degree studies] and wish to do so' which is appropriate for the 1980s and 1990s, rather than for the 1960s when it was first formulated.

All this discussion of the student who never came or might have come, lies behind much of the thinking of the Advisory Council for Adult and Continuing Education, and informs some passages in its response to the DES document, *Higher Education in the 1990s*. For it says, 'We think that the fundamental issue facing the educational system as a whole, and higher education in particular, is the urgent need for a transition from a "front end" model based upon full-time initial higher education for a relative few to an "open ended" model based upon the continuing or recurrent provision of full-time and part-time further and higher education for all who by virtue of ability, experience and motivation are able to benefit from it regardless of age'. It goes on, 'It is implicit in our proposals that admission and selection methods should provide alternatives to formal qualification requirements taking into account all types of relevant experiences.'

That looks towards a redefinition of the Robbins formula, one which could both put higher education at the service of a wider range of people drawn from every section of our population, and provide higher education with a new sense of direction and purpose. This book explores what such an attempt at redefining the Robbins formula can mean in practice for individuals and institutions.

In the eighteen years since the publication of the Robbins Report hundreds of thousands of young men and women have benefited from its recommendations about increasing the numbers of places for first degree study. In those same eighteen years, economic and social developments have changed the context in which higher education offers its services. The changes have been so great that there now seems to be something of a mis-match between the institutions offering the places and many of the individuals who might fill them. Whether, had more heed been given to some of the other views expressed by the Robbins Committee, that could be said now, it is impossible to say. What is now required for the last twenty years of the twentieth century, is that a better match should be made between what the colleges and universities provide and the individuals who may wish to use it.

3

Tomorrow's Students

Consistently, ever since the Robbins Committee was established in response to anxieties that able young people were being denied higher education because there were not enough places, the declared policy has been to make degree studies more widely available. Just as consistently, the results have been that available opportunities have been used not much more widely. The expansion has been broadly more of the same kinds of study, and more of the same kinds of students. Yet the intention of the policy remains: higher education ought to be providing for a wider range of the population than at present. The most promising future which higher education now needs has to be found in turning that policy into practice. To do so means recognizing that the lives many people lead do not fit easily alongside the traditional three or four year continuous residential courses. If higher education is to provide its services for all who wish to use them, and that is its proper future, the provision has to be altered, adding other possibilities for study.

Part-time study; periodic study, where results from courses over a period of years accumulate towards the eventual award of a degree; the transfer of those results from one institution to another; study programmes provided through a combination of formal teaching, home study supported by tapes and video tapes as well as programmed learning and study guides; alternative ways of becoming eligible for degree study; preparatory courses converted into exemption from parts of degree programmes; courses available throughout the calendar year, in every part of the country: all these seem far removed from the present provision of courses of higher education, except through the Open University. They may seem not quite so far away as proposals for admitting to higher education some of those who at present are deemed 'unqualified', and for planning individual study programmes between student and academic to fit the student's particular requirements, taking into account what the student can demonstrate that he or she has already mastered; or as far as asking industrial and commercial staff to contribute to higher education teaching as partners of institutional academic staff, because of the strength of their company's educational activities. But it can all fit readily into higher education.

Nothing is ever quite what it seems in any educational matter, especially in England. It is perfectly possible to produce examples, even if modified, of each one of these facilities – they are no more than an extension of present practices. Applicants can be admitted without formal qualifications. Students from other colleges and universities can also be admitted with full remission of course on the basis of previous results. Preparatory courses for degree work are taught. Independent study based on a student's own proposals is available in some institutions. Part-time degree courses are provided and some academic work can be completed substantially at home. Some staff members of industrial and commercial concerns do contribute to the teaching of degree programmes. But in no sense can any such examples be generalized into a normal part of higher education provision. Many of them depend on the personal initiative of individual academic staff. What may be the practice in a department in one institution may seem anathema to a similar department elsewhere. So the case rests: there is a sharp contrast between the normal provision available to potential students in higher education and the range of possibilities given above.

This contrast between teaching and taught exists because

institutions have not adapted their ways to the changes in social and economic life which have taken place around them. The changes have been dramatic. The world has disappeared in which office and professional workers led one sort of employment life, more or less from nine to five, and the rest of the working population worked longer hours, often with shift work as a condition of employment, with shorter (and unpaid) holidays. Government legislation to protect employers and employees, and statutory requirements for holidays with pay, have altered that. The introduction of flexible working hours for many people is another indication of the way things have changed, both at the place of work and in the circumstances of employees.

The strong drive towards house ownership, coupled with the problems of finding suitably-priced housing, has led many to make their homes far from their places of work. That creates a different pattern of travelling to work, making it increasingly inappropriate for everyone to keep the same hours. The improvement in transport services also means that long distance travel is an accepted feature of working life. There have been changes, too, in family life. More women are in regular employment. Significant numbers of married couples are either delaying their children or deciding not to have children at all, making a considerable difference to the rhythm and style of domestic life. In many households, running the house and caring for children is more evidently a shared responsibility now and one which extends to financial responsibilities. Just as flexi-time within a full-time job is one way of adjusting working conditions to those of the individual, so flexi-job is another. The drop-out student who made enough to live on through pottery or weaving and odd jobs to collect more money, with unemployment benefit as a stable income, was always more of a fiction than a typical example of a way of life for a significant number. There has, nevertheless, been a shift in attitudes to work. What were considered as 'manual' tasks are no longer the exclusive province of manual workers. There is not the same stigma attached to changing careers even where the change is from white-collar jobs to blue-collar. Side benefits can be as important as regular earnings: such as shorter working hours, longer holidays, relaxed conditions. Many people now want their lives to control their work rather than the other way round. It is all the natural accompaniment to the rising standards of living which are the normal expectation now for most households, with all manner of labour-saving appliances in the home, habitual travel by car, holidays abroad as a matter of course.

No such dramatic changes can be cited to characterize higher education, except the expansion of numbers. It can be said, of course, that it was precisely this role which the Open University was intended to fulfil.[1] For many whose lives have been affected by the kinds of changes mentioned there is no doubt that the Open University has enabled them to achieve their dreams, of graduating having studied subjects of their own choice from a relatively wide range of courses. But in two vital respects the Open University has not filled that role completely. Writing in *Trends*[2] as Chancellor of the University Lord Asa Briggs says that less than 20 per cent of each entry comes from manual workers, that only three out of every ten manual workers complete the course and graduate, and that they take longer to complete their studies than most others. He compares this with 31.4 per cent of the total 1971 entry who were teachers, and shows that seven out of ten teachers did graduate, and faster than others. So if part of the hopes for the kind of service the Open University would provide was that it would encourage precisely those social and economic groups which either were not making use of the possibilities for which they were formally qualified, or were unqualified and ineligible for degree study in existing institutions, then it appears that they have been largely disappointed.

[1] Walter Perry, *Open University*, Milton Keynes: Open University Press, 1976.
[2] Spring 1980.

There is another way in which the Open University has not fulfilled the role required by many. Perhaps it cannot because of the nature of the service it provides. Despite the excellence of its courses, planned down to the last detail and presented in book form and on television and radio with consummate professionalism, often a model for teachers everywhere, there is one missing element in the experience of learning it offers for many. That is regular contact with fellow students and tutors. The tutorial arrangements which are made in regions, the phone calls made by students to tutors and the summer school attendance requirements are of course significant attempts to compensate for this missing element in tuition. Within the terms of provision and its finances it is difficult to see how it could provide more classroom opportunities than it does. But for many this is a serious obstacle, notably for many teachers. Despite the large numbers of them who have graduated through the Open University, there are significant numbers who wish to study as part of their professional development and say they would prefer to follow an Open University course, but do not do so. Instead they attend part-time courses in colleges, polytechnics and universities as a second-best choice because they value the experience of weekly meetings with their peers. There is something about the weekly class meeting together with fellow students which they find supporting, encouraging and a source of learning in addition to whatever teaching is provided.[1] Now if that is true for numbers of teachers who are thoroughly familiar with the ways of study, it would not be surprising if many manual workers found this an equally strong deterrent. Indeed, anyone with experience of teaching adults would expect this to be the case. They need continual individual encouragement and support until they gain some self-confidence about their capacity to study. The onus is thus thrown more firmly on the various institutions of higher education which in theory, at any rate, are

[1] Norman Evans, *Preliminary Evaluation of the In-Service B.Ed. Degree*, Windsor: NFER, 1981.

capable of providing precisely what the Open University cannot.

The general lack of response by universities, polytechnics and colleges is in some ways surprising, given the proliferation of institutions in the last fifteen years. Partly this is because of the pecking order problem. Although polytechnics were intended to develop substantial provision for part-time degree courses – that was supposed to be one of their distinguishing marks – until recently they have seemed anxious to concentrate on full-time courses. Quite apart from the financial advantages, this was largely because evidence of burgeoning full-time courses was the most direct means of demonstrating that polytechnics were the academic equals of universities. Something of the same attitude has led the most recently established colleges and institutes of higher education to strive for the largest possible number of students on full-time courses. In that way they too could demonstrate their teaching prowess at an academic level. In terms of strict equivalence of effective teaching for first degrees, they may well be correct. In terms of providing a service to the population it could be a seductive cul-de-sac. There were other opportunities – one was sub-degree work. But interested in pursuing the greater prestige of teaching degrees, the general tendency of polytechnics and the larger colleges of art and technology was to transfer lower level courses to other further education colleges. When the colleges and institutes were first trying to work out their new future from the re-organization of teacher education, they gave scant attention to the possibilities of teaching courses which were not award-bearing with a degree or diploma as the final qualification. For both groups of institutions this may prove to have been an expensive mistake.

The intention was that the polytechnics should teach first degrees at the same level as universities in courses that would be more concerned with the application rather than the acquisition of knowledge (which someone clearly thought characterized the provision of universities). This has not happened because it was a misconceived notion in the first place.[1] It rests on the assumption that university education was not concerned with vocational preparation, an assumption which has always been unfounded. What has happened is that, within their full-time courses, universities have kept their vocational preparation in step with the changes in the world of the professions, in management and employment. Inevitably, university provision has tended to move towards the applied courses which were supposed to characterize the polytechnics while polytechnics have developed full-time courses like universities. So the division of function between the two sets of institutions simply has not worked out. Given the changes in economic and social life and their effects on careers and occupational opportunities, this is not at all surprising. Indeed it makes the policy for the creation of the polytechnics seem somewhat naive. But it is a clear illustration of the problems of trying to adjust higher education provision[2] where the conception of first-degree work as three and four year full-time courses predominates.

What is so very unfortunate about this lack of development along the lines which were intended for polytechnics is that precious time has been lost in establishing general acceptance of part-time study. This is not to underestimate the importance of the part-time degree courses which polytechnics have launched, often with considerable success. The issue is the emphasis which institutions have given to their development. It takes a comparatively long time to plan, staff and allocate resources for the development of any degree courses. Now with financial constraints tightening on local education authorities and on the DES, it will be disproportionately difficult to develop new part-time courses for the foreseeable future, however strong the case for starting them. Yet this is the most compelling need, and some twenty years have been lost in answering it.

[1] Peter Scott, *What Future for Higher Education?*, London: Fabian Tract 465, 1975.
[2] Stephen Bragg and Harold Silver in *Education Beyond School*, edited by Norman Evans, London: Grant McIntyre, 1980; Charles Carter, *The Future of Higher Education*, Oxford: Basil Blackwell, 1980.

The comparison with the comprehensive reorganization of secondary education is instructive. There, the major effort has gone into the administrative requirements for establishing a new system. Not enough systematic attention has been paid to the kinds of educational provision the comprehensive schools were expected to make. In some ways this is predictable; it is so much easier to attend to the major structural issues than to the day to day requirements, even though they alone justify the structural reorganization. In the case of the comprehensive schools this imbalance of effort has been in part responsible for the current dissatisfaction with some secondary schooling. It is connected with the Great Debate, so called, which featured in the Labour government's period of office from 1974 to 1979. It may not be too far-fetched either to suggest that it has something to do with the latest Tory response to comprehensive schools through legislation for the Assisted Places scheme, which can only be seen as a vote of no confidence in the capacity of comprehensive schools to provide for the most able.

In higher education a major effort has gone into expanding the system since 1963, and since 1966 into what was intended to be a major effort to expand the range of courses and ways of study, through polytechnics. The colleges and institutes of higher education hardly featured in this. Although a significant major government initiative had to go into reorganizing teacher education (and so incidentally creating the third category of higher education institutions), and despite the intentions declared for them in the White Paper on Education, *A Framework for Expansion* (where it was somewhat grandly stated that they were to join the family of higher education), there is no evidence to show that the Government ever seriously tried to use them for expanding the provision. Had it done so, the story of higher education unfolding now might be very different. A clear brief and a binding one to either the polytechnics or the colleges and institutions for certain kinds of development could conceivably be making some difference now. Had polytechnics and colleges considered what different kinds of service they could have provided without duplicating university provision, then part-time and sub-degree courses could well have become a significant feature. It is not unlikely that other developments would have followed. For example, some form of credit accumulation allowing for periodic rather than sequential study would have been a natural outcome. Students, and more important potential students, would have viewed what higher education offered in an altered light. This is the crux – what we have instead is a mismatch. What could have been, has not happened. Horizons are not much wider; they are more or less the same.

There has been another influence bearing on institutions which has in some ways tended to narrow horizons rather than widen course provision: the professions. Professional bodies have become increasingly important as controllers of educational activities. Historically, they have been overseers of the conduct of their members, and part of that control has been exercised through establishing the qualification which intending professionals must acquire. That has always been a highly desirable and, indeed, necessary form of control since it serves to ensure acceptable standards in the professional services and is a protection for the public.

However, the complications of professional practice have grown. Increasing mastery of technical matters is required; continual additions are being made to statutory requirements in bewildering succession and with overwhelming speed. In response entry requirements to professions tended to be formalized and become more prescriptive, attempting to ensure adequate standards. As a result, when a professional body considers the courses offered by universities, polytechnics and colleges as preparation for professional practice, it has been increasingly concerned that the syllabuses should correspond to what they consider are the essential knowledge and skills members require.

Two particular tensions can arise. One comes from the different perspectives often held by scholars and professionals in the field. Sometimes it can be the academics who are responsible for the narrowing of view – a complaint sometimes made by students about their courses, criticizing too much concentration upon the abstract and theoretical aspect of the study, without direct reference to its professional application. Sometimes the narrowing comes from the opposite source. If too much insistence is placed on mastering those aspects which have immediate application, then the possibility of setting the professional work in a wider context of understanding can be lost. To characterize the contrast, it is as if there were a choice between a thoroughly professional automaton who knew all the answers but had little idea of their origin or of the kinds of adaptations which might have professional significance for individuals and a scholarly dreamer full of ideas but with little notion of how to use them to benefit others. Somewhere in between the two lies the conception of the educated professional who has acquired some wisdom from understanding the human context in which his professional services are used.

The other tension comes from the students. For most, the prime interest is to qualify and secure the best appointment. They naturally tend to question the value of any parts of a course which do not appear to be helping them directly towards that goal. Elements of study which may help to prepare students as educated rather than narrow professionals can easily get a hostile reception. Given the consultative procedures which exist now for most courses, to provide opportunities for students to tell their tutors their views of the courses, there can be considerable tension over content. These tensions can be reduced when some of the teaching staff in academic institutions have spent time in professional practice. The academic institution, the profession and the students can all benefit. Indeed it can be so beneficial that it is surprising it is not more frequent, and on a part-time basis is well.

Professional control can also bear strongly on the studies of those who hope to join a profession at an earlier stage. Some professions specify strictly the combination of 'O' and 'A' Level passes required to become eligible for subsequent admission. To the extent that such specifications are narrow, then again there is a tendency for professional influence to limit the studies of students. One significant feature of this for higher education in general is that it narrows the access to the professions. Another, and far more important because of its pervasive influence, is that it entrenches more widely and firmly than ever the requirement of formal qualifications at every level. Since gaining formal qualifications usually starts at school, and since the lack of them is one of the most significant deterrents for many who leave school early from considering themselves and their potential against the possibilities offered by higher education, it is bound to serve as a further obstacle to those who came from the manual worker classes. There is little or no experience to guide them at home, and often what guidance is available from school, college of further education or career advisers is not offered with an empathetic understanding of the inquirer's perceptions of higher education. Rather than encouraging participation in higher education from the widest possible groups of the population, the general effect of the increasingly powerful role of professional bodies can be to discourage it. This is particularly important to older men and women who may be as competent as professionally qualified people. If they do not have the required qualifications they are not even eligible for studying to become professionally qualified. It is another example of how the higher education system is somewhat out of joint with adults who may want to study. Part of the future for higher education lies in serving more adult learners. They cannot be served if insufficient attention is paid to their particular requirements.

There is another gloss to this essential point about older students. Their requirements for learning are not necessarily the same for their children. Psychologists of all persuasions have been paying increasing attention to the significance of the different stages which can be identified within the span of human development. No doubt the age and stage of our society is simply being reflected by these notable preoccupations. As the stresses on individuals increase, so does the drive intensify to find ways of explaining what it is that is happening to us. Alterations in family patterns, in occupational patterns, in the relationships between men and women and the roles they undertake, in the relatively high level of expectations of standards of living, of mobility of persons and homes, all are creating new conditions of life for many. Since both personal and professional efficiency and effectiveness are at stake, with incalculable consequences for individual well-being, not surprisingly, social science is paying determined attention to the genesis, function and results of these complex developments. There must be consequences of all this concern for higher education.

What are they? Where can we find examples of courses, teaching methods and modes of study consciously developed according to what the psychologists are beginning to help us understand about the correlations between the stages we all experience, but perhaps do not always recognize?

It is here that the seriousness of the mismatch becomes so much more evident. There is criticism enough of the schools; that is not the concern of this book. But the consequences for higher education are, and it is important to pick up one or two significant points. They relate to potential students of all ages, who ignore higher education at present. A striking difference seems to occur between what are accepted as the best ways of teaching young children, and the teaching offered to many of them in secondary schools. Carefully prepared and organized inquiry and discovery approaches to learning characterize so much good teaching of younger children and adolescents. Materials are presented, problems are set, answers are tested as hypotheses, the process is repeated on different materials, some concepts are grasped, some rules are learned which apply to working in the discipline, and some level of understanding is reached. That is what can happen at best, and in many infant and junior schools it happens in fact. The authority for what is to be learned does not come from the teacher, but from the nature of what is being studied. Unfortunately there are many pupils who are not taught in this way in secondary schools. Somehow it can seem as if the steady course of human development is being ignored. Material is often presented as immutable fact, as information which has to be accepted, memorized and reproduced on the authority of the teacher. So often if there is understanding, through use of information in that way, in other words if anything has been learnt, it is more a matter of chance than of conscious design. At the very time when young people are trying out their own authority the learning they are expected to master is presented as something externally imposed: '[I came] to doubt whether . . . an overdevelopment of the critical faculty would not have been at least as dangerous as its underdevelopment.'[1] Small wonder that so many of them resist being taught this way.

This is a criticism, nevertheless, of a system of secondary schooling which has been deliberately reorganized on comprehensive lines, so that the best opportunities for learning can be offered to all young people up to the age of sixteen with the hope of encouraging them to go beyond that education level. Not enough professional effort has gone into trying to improve what the schools are there to do for their pupils day by day, compared with the effort which went into reorganizing the system. It is all very understandable but thoroughly regrettable. Professionally it is the far more difficult task to attempt these pedagogical matters, but what counts ultimately in schools is what the pupils and their parents think of the schooling provided. What they think is primarily a response to the quality of teaching. If it is felt that there is a mismatch between the pupils and the learning they are expected to accomplish, the risks are that the system as a whole will be dismissed as irrele-

[1] Vera Brittain, *Testament of Youth*, London: Fontana, 1979, pp. 378.

vant or useless, and it is bound to affect their perceptions of higher education. Unhappily, this is just what happens all too frequently. More or less the same range of queries can be posed for higher education itself. If the Robbins precept had been taken seriously perhaps they could not be posed now: '. . . a vast mass whose performance both at entry and higher education and beyond depends greatly on how they have lived and been taught beforehand.' But they can. The case here is that the failure to follow Robbins is partially responsible for the persistently low response from young people in social classes III, IV and V to institutions of higher education.

This mismatch for the 18-plus students, is ever more pressing for higher education when it looks as if increasing numbers of students are likely to be older adults. The older adults who may turn to higher education are so much more than adults in law. Emotionally, intellectually, physically, they are at different stages from 18-plus students. The question is how much of the content of courses, the conduct of classes, lectures and seminars and tutorials, and the devising of examinations is designed consciously and deliberately for the knowledge and skills of the students following the course? It will vary from discipline to discipline of course, but it is not the fundamental principle on which academic courses are planned today.

When the question is posed alongside some of the characteristics of human development which are related to ways and purposes of learning at different stages of life, its significance for higher education becomes obvious. Consider a fifty-five year old man as he faces the fact that his children have left home and are independent, that he may be required to retire early, and that he has some twenty to thirty years ahead of him in which to live out the rest of his life with a wife who does not really have enough to do. What motivates him to higher education will be very different from the desire to study of a thirty-year-old man who senses that he needs further study if he is to make the best of career opportunities for the benefit of his growing family and ambitious wife. Then there is the thirty-year-old housewife who had her children early and now has some sense of freedom from insistent domestic demands and wants to strike out on her own and enjoy the opportunities which in some ways she regrets not taking when she was eighteen. She will have very different intentions from the woman in her twenties with young babies who wants the assurance she anticipates will come from following her own interests to a greater depth so that she can feel that she is keeping up with her husband and satisfying him. Different again will be the objective of a fifty-year-old woman who realizes that she would be wise to prepare herself for the changes which will come when her husband retires.

In so many ways the interests these potential students bring are so different from those it is assumed 18 year olds have in their studies. Some of those assumptions about 18 year olds may not be well-founded; even so, there can be little doubt that if teachers were to consider the range of interests represented in the random selection of potential students just given, they might well adopt different approaches, selecting different material, and indeed conceiving different kinds of courses from those they give to the traditional 18-plus student. This is also often talked of in schools: that teachers should be aware of the heterogeneity of any class, and should arrange their teaching to fit. When set against the range of personal interests and stages of development represented in any group of adult applicants, it poses fundamental problems for teachers in higher education.

For example, the man who turns to higher education for some kind of re-training wants to gain a qualification and the recognition that goes with it. He will be looking for the assurance that he is getting the knowledge he wants because it is authenticated by some external authority, either by the teacher himself, or by a professional body. He is interested primarily in acquiring for himself a status or sense of status derived from meeting the expectations of others. By contrast, the woman who is seeking to prepare for her husband's retirement has very different interests. She is concerned to deepen her understanding of herself and the knowledge she seeks is likely to be most satisfying when it enables her to acquire fresh insights and becomes the authority for her own learning. These two students would best be served by contrasting styles of teaching.

Any study of the curriculum of a university, polytechnic or college in terms of the stages of development of its students would almost certainly reveal something of the kind of mismatch which is frequently characterized in the teaching of adolescents at school. It is hardly surprising, then, that the perceptions of many potential students are what they are: that higher education has nothing for them.

Exceptional teachers are skilled in varying their approaches to take account of the differences they recognize in their students. Their success is often founded on this and appreciation from students merely reflects it. These students will have experienced what can be done in lectures, classes, seminars and discussion groups. But many more are not so lucky. This is the essential point; the number of the unlucky can be reduced if institutions and tutors are convinced that there is an important academic job to be done in re-designing courses with these specific requirements in mind.

This story of the failure of the expansion of higher education to include significant numbers of those for whom the expansion was intended can also begin at a different starting point: in 1944. The expansion can be seen as the inevitable and necessary consequence of the 1944 Education Act. Secondary education for all meant opening the full range of educational opportunities to the entire school aged population. For a short time it was possible to assume that the new system was working to great advantage. The 11-plus controversy changed that assumption. It became clear that the selection procedure for secondary education really meant selecting a varying proportion of boys and girls for grammar schools, from 10 to 30 per cent according to which part of the country they lived in, but with the near certainty that there would be a 10 per cent error in the border line dividing those who were awarded grammar school places and those who were not. Comprehensive schools were introduced in part to avoid this thoroughly unacceptable margin of error, and so reintroduce the equality of opportunity which was supposed to have been the basis of the provision.

In the meantime, however, what had happened was that the more formal academic achievements, measured through examination results, had become the hallmark of successful secondary education for most parents, and so for their children, as well as for a very large number of teachers. Those who were not successful according to this criterion came to think of themselves as failures. In a bizarre way, equality of opportunity, far from giving encouragement to the minority of school pupils, seemed to demonstrate, even confirm, their lack of ability which did not and could not stop at the school level. Success beyond that became identified with higher education. It is here that the small part the children of social classes III, IV and V have played in higher education becomes so important. The kind of success which many of these children achieved at school following their selection for grammar places seemed to encourge them towards a life in higher education and beyond which, according to what they gathered from their teacher mentors, did not seem to fit very happily with what they thought of themselves. In a word, most of the able children from these socio-economic classes simply did not want to join what appeared to them to be an elite. Some did but so many of the able ones did not.[1]

If this is true of the very able children from manual workers' homes, then how much more is it likely to have been felt by other children from the same kind of background who, while not so able, were perfectly capable of meeting the intellectual demands. Friendship bonds in home neighbourhoods reinforced these views. If grammar school boys and girls turned down the chances of going to university or college, because they preferred to take a job locally, their example was bound to be a powerful

[1] J. W. B. Douglas, J. M. Ross and H. R. Simpson, *All Our Future*, London: Peter Davies, 1968; A. H. Halsey, A. F. Heath and J. M. Ridge, *Origins and Destinations: Family, Class and Education in Modern Britain*, Oxford: OUP, 1980.

influence on their friends who were attending technical or secondary modern schools where so often there were opportunities for carrying studies up to the pre-higher education stage, and so into it. Time and time again teachers in all these secondary schools found examples of able young people who for such variety of reasons, simply were not able to benefit from the opportunities which had been created. And there is the rub.

This goes back to the other side of Robbins – that higher education needed to take into account the manner of living and schooling which had been experienced by the 'vast mass' when it came to offering its services to them. Unfortunately, it has not. There is no other way of accounting for the gap which exists between the position and condition of so many of the population and the way higher education offers its services. It is not a question of people's ability, of their being incapable of studying at degree level. It is simply that one does not engage with the other. As long as the policy remains of providing a higher education system which is there to be used by those with the ability and who 'wish to do so', then the responsibility for putting that policy into practice remains to a large extent with the institutions.

Home circumstances have changed. Family roles have altered. Family planning has affected family structures. Developments in transport and the credit card economy have changed people's ways of life. Work circumstances have changed. What people want cannot any more be measured by wage and salary figures and these domestic economic and social developments affect the attitudes of eighteen year olds who have been predominantly the traditional students, just as they can govern those of older people, when it comes to looking at their relationship to higher education. These factors present institutions of higher education simultaneously with two sets of demands if they are to put public policy into practice. The courses of study, and how they can be studied, both need to be designed and planned in full recognition of these changing

4

Today's Students in the USA

Despite all the differences between higher education provision in the United States of America and in Britain there are at present some important similarities. They serve as a common base from which each country is attempting to resolve common problems. But the differences between the established systems in the two countries mean that American approaches to seeking solutions contrast singularly with Britain's. Those approaches are the principal concern of this chapter. In Britain the critical task for higher education is to find a better match between institutions and potential students. Much can be learned from American experience where matching is at the heart of their tradition.

Demography and technology have a lock grip on higher education planning and provision in each country. The prospective decline in the number of 18 year olds is just as pronounced in the US as in Britain. It is commonly expressed in terms of the ratios of first-grade children in school (aged 6) to eleventh graders (aged 17). According to a representative of the State Board of Education for Wisconsin in 1979 the ratio was one to two. For Pennsylvania and Massachusetts it was one to more than two. Within twenty-five years it is estimated that the overall number of eleventh graders nationally will be down by 25 per cent. During the 1980s the number of 18-plus young people (the largest source of higher education recruitment hitherto) will decline until it is three quarters to half its present size, varying between different states in the Union. The consequences are obvious. The very size of the provision can make them acute. In 1977/78 there were 3086 institutions[1] of higher education in all counting 160 universities, 1775 four-year institutions offering the full range of undergraduate work and usually some graduate studies as well, and 1151 two-year institutions, mainly community colleges. Many of the private universities and colleges (1618 in all: 65 universities, 1318 four-year institutions and 235 two-year colleges) which are independent of state government and not directly funded by public finance are worrying about recruitment. So are many of the institutions in the state systems (1468 in all: 95 universities, 457 four-year institutions and 916 two-year colleges) which were expanded during the 1960s to take account of the increasing numbers then seeking places.

As fees rise, carried upwards with the general inflationary increases in prices, institutions without substantial endowments or state support are increasingly vulnerable. In each of the past few years, some have closed. As public expenditure gets caught off balance between inflation and taxation, so state legislatures seek to restrict their education budgets: where recruitments do not seem able to support all the institutions in a state system, then they come under threat. The temptation is to lower academic standards to boost recruitment. The story and the tensions are becoming familiar to some institutions in Britain.

In each country technological developments are having a profound effect on the social and economic lives of its members. Education and training as a continuous process from school to the end of a higher education course as a preparation for a lifetime career is now seriously deficient. Re-training once or more during a working career is now the common calculation by

[1] National Center for Educational Statistics, *Digest*, Washington D.C., 1979.

employers of all kinds. This applies to the professions just as much as to production and service industries.

It can apply equally to those who work in offices, and to those on the factory floor. These trends affect higher education in many ways, but two in particular need noting straight away. First, new demands are going to be made on higher education to use its resources for many kinds of re-training and, indeed, are already being made extensively. Second, industrial and commercial employers are so conscious of their need to keep abreast of any technological developments which relate to their own field of activities that many are responding by undertaking the re-education and re-training for themselves. Every step they make along that path takes them further towards becoming educational institutions in their own right. That raises the question of the relationship between the two sets of institutions, colleges and universities who think of themselves as formal education providers, supplying well-prepared personnel for employers, and industrial and commercial concerns who may have complained about the service they received from the formal educational institutions, but are coming to think of themselves as their own major resource for education and training. This development of employers as educators is probably more pronounced in the US than in Britain, but broadly speaking the implications are the same. So much in common; beyond that, all is contrast. This is where the investigation of matching in the US must begin.

One of the few things which can be said with confidence about American society is that it is heterogeneous. Size alone means that, for a country which stretches from Atlantic to Pacific, about every pattern of living and working can be found somewhere. Just as it contains a wide range of ethnic origins, with nearly every race on earth represented, so the education provision is equally varied. In any community with a college or university there is a variety of ways in which its services can be used. As well as providing full-time study, there are usually many part-time courses. Sometimes it is quite simply that

47

classes provided for full-time students are opened to part-time students. There are specially provided courses offered within evening programmes and week-end colleges, and summer semesters are organized as what are in effect fourth, and sometimes, fifth, terms of study within an academic year. Increasingly, in more remote parts, distance learning facilities of tapes, discs, video tapes and study guides are available for those who cannot travel easily to college. This variety of possibilities enables students of all ages to fit their studies to suit them. The traditional full-time 18-plus student can reduce the four-year period of studies usually taken for a baccalaureate degree by many additional summer semester courses. Older men or women in employment can take some courses in the evening programme, some from the daytime programme if they can be fitted in, and some from the summer semester courses. There is an almost infinite number of combinations, and all work within a system of credit accumulation where the award of a degree depends on the satisfactory completion of the required number of courses, usually between 32 and 40 sixteen-week courses in certain specified categories.

This timetabling is only one way in which the provision is as varied as the students' conditions; credit transfer is another. This is a means whereby courses completed satisfactorily at one institution can be accepted at another as if they had been taught for its degree programme. It enables students to study in a college or university, store the result of that study in a personal 'academic bank', and offer it for acceptance in another institution. This credit transfer is by no means automatic, nor is it always available. Of course, institutions have their own rules on time limits, the maximum permissible time between periods of study. But in most areas in the US there are some institutions which accept students on this basis.

It is important to realize that these provisions apply to post-graduate work as well as undergraduate studies, although less so, especially for transfer. Some institutions allow applicants with a baccalaureate degree to study for a Master's through the same mixture of full-time and part-time study. Again, there are time limits. For older students with domestic and occupational responsibilities, this is of the greatest significance. It means that a vast proportion of provision for higher education study is specifically organized and administered so as to make it as widely available as possible. In 1977, sixty per cent of graduate students in the USA were studying part-time.[1] To describe this provision as full- or part-time study is far too limiting. Studies can be interrupted more or less at the wish of students. Periodic study is not only possible but very frequent. Thus the relationship between studying and earning a living, or just living, can be varied substantially to suit the circumstances of the individual. In many ways it simply reproduces in higher education many of the characteristics of America's commercial world. Shops of all kinds are open for far longer periods than is usually the case in Britain; the determining factor seems to be simply the presence of potential customers. Similarly, if enough students wish to study in a particular way, then institutions are likely to arrange their provisions to fit.

There is one compelling reason for this set of arrangements – money. Whatever the status of the university or college, whether private or state, the financial basis is the same: students pay for their education through fees. Customarily, state institutions charge lower fees than private schools and colleges. State institutions themselves usually charge lower fees for students who are 'In State' (resident within the state boundaries or having their homes there if they are still living with their parents) than for 'Out of State' students. There are a number of state and federally-funded schemes for assisting students from lower-income homes. And there is a federally-backed student loan scheme. All these factors make a difference to the amounts of fee money students are required to pay and to the timing of their payments in the case of loans. But they in no way diminish the force of the fact that students pay their own fees. One

[1] National Center for Educational Statistics, *Digest*, Washington D.C., 1979.

consequence is that both students and institutions tend to think of students registering for courses as customers in a commercial transaction, rather than clients dependent upon what institutions offer. So the variety of modes and levels of study and of courses is a calculated response to the market conditions of potential students as the institution perceives them. Some may offer traditional academic programmes, others highly innovative ones, depending on the institution's view of itself.

This is epitomized by the universally accepted pattern of study, 'Putting yourself through school'. It is part of the everyday vocabulary of post-secondary education in the US for parents and their children, almost irrespective of income. Very large numbers of young people will study for some of their time, and work for some of their time, to earn money towards the cost of their higher education. The work may be within the institution, in one of the student aid schemes, involving many different kinds of clerical, supervisory tasks as well as unskilled labour. It may be evening work in a local cinema or restaurant, or it may involve taking a full semester away to take on a full-time job. Just as with patterns of study, the variety is enormous, though necessarily limited by the economic conditions of the area. Whatever patterns students or potential students adopt, or are forced to adopt, if they are earning money to spend on fees for courses towards a degree, then they will tend to take some care in choosing what they buy. This is where credit transfer can be seen in context. It means that at the beginning of a four-year undergraduate course, many students will think of spending only two years in one institution with a clear view of taking a year away from their studies, doing something quite different, and then seeking entrance to a different institution which will accept their transferred credits, where they can then complete their degree. This principle of students paying their own fees lies at the core of educational institutions; they have a social purpose as well as an educational one. Neither can be achieved unless the institutions respond to the conditions of those sections of the population which wish to make use of them. It is that continuing responsiveness, seeking the most appropriate match between institutional provision and students' needs, which represents an attempt to find solutions to the problems posed by demography and technology.

Another development is equally important. In the mid 1960s, higher education in the US faced a different kind of crisis – not too few students but a large increase – as did most technological societies. In the US this fairly rapid move towards higher education becoming a mass rather than an elite provision was accompanied by an almost bewildering array of new courses. Larger numbers brought problems; they also provided opportunities for students. Many restive students of the 1960s protested about what and how they were taught. Many institutions responded by increasing the range of academic courses, and many academic staff seized the opportunities enthusiastically, although many still remain sceptical. The main thrust of this development was to try to produce courses that convinced students that they were relevant to their lives, both at the time of study and for the future, and to attempt to further this idea through involving students in activities related to theories of social change. All kinds of interdisciplinary courses appeared in attempts to bridge what students perceived as gaps between what they were being offered and what they wanted to do with their lives when they had completed their studies. Community Environmental Studies was one approach. Film, television and media courses generally represented a different approach, beginning with significant developments in society and then working backwards to making a systematic study of them as phenomena. Other social influences introduced Black Studies, Hispanic Studies and Women's Studies in turn.

Alongside these attempts at studying rapidly-changing social developments there came a different approach – field experience. The idea of learning through practical activity rather than through formal study has a respectable and well-founded basis. Learning through doing is now an accepted part of any schooling in theory, in the United States as in Great Britain. As Dewey

51

put it, 'there is an intricate and necessary relation between the process of actual experience and education.'[1] Field experience is based on that concept. It offered rich opportunities for an institution to provide students with the very kind of activity they complained was excluded from their campus studies. This was quite distinct from the long-established co-op (or sandwich) courses which have been offered throughout the country in science, engineering, law management and so on. Field experience outside co-op courses meant students spending periods within a degree programme in almost any activity which faculty members were prepared to accept as a valid and appropriate experience. Assignments of all kinds were arranged, either by the institutions on behalf of students or by students for themselves. Some were with state and federal agencies in social services, but just as frequently in government offices of all kinds. Some were attachments to elected politicians, working in their offices. Some were in voluntary agencies, others in commercial and industrial concerns. Periods spent abroad featured prominently. But usually there was one consistent factor – they all carried credit towards the award of the degree. The significance of this was that it institutionalized the notion that credit could be awarded for off-campus activities, of almost any kind.

This development converges with another. Some forty years ago the American Council for Education (ACE) introduced a system for awarding credit on the basis of course work undertaken by personnel in the armed forces. ACE now publishes guides for colleges which relate the content and level of attainment required in the Armed Forces' courses to those of college level courses, and recommend the credit institutions should consider awarding to applicants who have successfully completed those courses. There are three *Guides to the Evaluation of Educational Experiences in the Armed Forces*,[2] one for the Army, one for the Navy-Marine Coast Guard and one for the Air Force.

---

[1] John Dewey, *Experience and Education*, New York: Collier, 1963.
[2] ACE, Washington, D.C., 1976.

ACE now also publishes a *National Guide to Credit Recommendations for Noncollegiate Courses*,[1] which gives similar information and recommendations for courses offered by corporations and other civilian organizations. The New York Regents'[2] Programme of Noncollegiate Sponsored Instruction offers a similar service. Each guide makes clear the basis of its evaluation of a particular course, and emphasises that institutions have the responsibility, which they cannot share, for deciding whether to accept, modify, or reject any recommendation made. These developments rested on a clear principle; that it was academically acceptable for educational institutions to give formal recognition for all kinds of learning which men and women have acquired through study elsewhere.

Every developed country has prestigious institutions which will not be unduly troubled by demography, although they too can hardly evade the realities of the technological age in which their students will find their living. Nevertheless they will not be without troubles; since most major universities and colleges in the USA are private, they are worried by rapidly rising fees, at a time when rapidly rising inflation is squeezing the middle income groups from whom they have drawn so many students. At Harvard, for instance, the fees with residence for each student are not far off $10,000 each year. With taxation running at 30 per cent, that can mean a man earning a high income of $100,000 before tax could be spending one seventh of his after-tax income on higher education for one child. It is now relatively easy to find parents with a combined income of some $40,000 having to borrow to finance their children's higher education. The effect of these pressures on the academic calibre of an institution's recruitment has not so far been felt at full force. But it is small wonder that some private institutions are busy fundraising for scholarships for students from middle and lower income homes who are liable to be squeezed out of the system.

[1] ACE, Washington D.C., 1979.
[2] This is the body controlling higher education in the State of New York.

For the general run of higher education institutions however, recruitment is now a critical issue – the search for answers often focuses on adults as additional potential students. It is here that field experience and credit for noncollegiate courses hold such important implications. Yet both are potentially dangerous if used indiscriminately, because they could run counter to the preservation of academic standards without which higher education would fall into disrepute.

Of the two, the noncollegiate course work is the easier to accept, although the size of the undertaking alone makes it difficult to grasp. The starting point for both the American Council of Education and the New York Regents' was the belief that large numbers of adults were following courses provided by corporations, trade unions and voluntary agencies, reaching attainment levels equivalent to what they would have achieved had they been attending the same course at a college or university. They recognized that hundreds of thousands of military personnel were undertaking such courses each year, and that millions of other adults were also studying while being employed. Currently some two thousand colleges across the United States are making use of the ACE system for awarding credit for course work completed during military service. Further there are some five hundred colleges using the ACE and New York system of recommendations for credit towards degrees for course work offered by all the non-military bodies. In total, therefore, these two systems are dealing with a substantial amount of the college-level study in the USA which is conducted outside the formal education systems, and are bringing it within the fold of formally recognized and validated academic learning.

Both systems are based on a thorough syllabus review. Teams of academic evaluators will scrutinize a course offered by the Armed Forces, or by corporations, voluntary agencies, or trade unions, and compare it with courses offered in higher education in the same subject area. Having considered the content of the course, its duration and the attainment levels which typically can be expected from students who complete the course satisfactorily, they then make academic judgements; first, about its appropriateness as a course of study for a first degree programme; second, about the amount of credit the course could carry if it were offered as part of a college curriculum for its on-campus students. The judgements stand only as recommendations; it is up to the college to decide on the appropriateness of course content and credit value in the light of its own perception of academic standards and curricula. But, in making its own decisions, a college has the assurance of knowing that a thorough evaluation has been made by experienced members of higher education's academic community, and that there is no question of applicants who ask for this kind of previous study to be taken into account being given an easy route through to graduation.

The examples which follow (figures 1 and 2) show how the evaluation teams do their work to provide colleges and universities with evidence of what courses contain, and illustrate the recommendations which they feel able to make about validity and value in conventional academic terms.

Figure 1: Three U.S. Army 'Course Exhibits' with credit recommendations, from the *Guide to the Evaluation of Educational Experiences in the Armed Forces.*

Quantitative Techniques in Materiel Acquisition and Integrated Logistics Support
Design Management
    Course Number: None.
    Location: Logistics Management Center, Ft. Lee. VA.
    Length: 2 weeks (73 hours).
    Exhibit Dates: 10/75–Present.
       Objectives: To train officers and civilian personnel in the concepts of quantitative techniques employed by the system engineer and logistics planner in the application of integrated logistics support.

Instruction: Lecture-conferences, practical exercises, and computer simulations in the application of integrated logistics support management. Topics include concepts, principles, and policies of materiel acquisition and logistics management; quantitative techniques in materiel acquisition and logistics support; analytical techniques related to decision making and cost effectiveness; and trade-off determinations using logistic parameters.

Credit Recommendation: In the upper division baccalaureate category, 2 semester hours in materiel acquisition process and support systems; in the graduate degree category, 1 semester hour in materiel acquisition process and support systems.

Economic Analysis for Decision Making
   Course Number: 7A-710.
   Location: Management Engineering Training.
   Agency, Rock Island, IL.
   Length: 2 weeks (77 hours).
   Exhibit Dates: 9/72–Present.

Objectives: To provide the concepts and economics analysis techniques for evaluating cost impacts on an organization prior to final management decisions.

Instruction: Lecture, conferences, practical exercises, programmed instruction, and case study to include management and decision making, cost estimating techniques, time value money, basic methods for comparison of alternatives, equipment replacement, regulating policies, and cost-benefit analysis.

Credit Recommendation: In the upper-division baccalaureate category, 3 semester hours in financial management.

Engineered Performance Standards (EPS) for Facilities Engineering Estimators
   Course Number: AMETA-11.

Location: Management Engineering Training.
Agency, Rock Island, IL.
Length: 2 weeks (78 hours).
Exhibit Dates: 7/74–Present.

Objectives: To provide a working knowledge of engineered performance standards for planning and estimating work relative to facilities engineering.

Instruction: Thorough development of skill in application of standard data for real-property maintenance applications. Covers the fundamentals of general data available in the areas of job preparation, craft allowance and travel time, fundamentals of craft data, job phasing, data presentation, and the procedures for applying engineering standards using job planning sheets and monographs.

Credit Recommendation: In the upper-division baccalaureate category, 2 semester hours in public works administration.

Figure 2: Three 'Course Exhibits' with credit recommendations for Corporation Courses. From ACE's *National Guide to Credit Recommendations for Noncollegiate Courses;* the courses were given by the General Electric Company.

Management Accounting
(Management Cost Accounting)
Location: Philadelphia, PA.
Length: 34 hours (17 weeks).
Dates: January 1971–Present.

Objective: To provide students with an understanding of cost accounting as a quantitative device for use by managers in selecting and researching objectives.

Instruction: General cost accounting concepts; job order costs; standard costs; process costs; direct costing and government contract costing. Involves lecture, discussion, and homework projects.

Credit Recommendation: In the upper division baccalaureate category, 3 semester hours in Accounting.

Materials Engineering I
  Location: Valley Forge Space Center, Valley Forge, PA.
  Length: 60 hours (30 weeks).
  Dates: September 1974–Present.
  Objective: To provide students with an introduction to materials science.

  Instruction: Principles underlying structure, properties, and behavior of engineering materials, including metals, ceramics, and polymers. Bonding; crystal structure; defect structure; alloying; mechanical; electronic and magnetic properties in relation to structure; phase equilibrium; phase transformation. Instruction is chiefly lecture.

  Credit Recommendation: In the lower division baccalaureate/associate degree category, 3 semester hours in engineering.

Modern Structural Analysis I
(Survey of Topics in Structural Analysis)
  Location: Philadelphia and Valley Forge, PA.
  Length: 60 hours (30 weeks).
  Dates: September 1977–Present.
  Objective: To provide design engineers with a survey of selected topics in structural analysis.

  Instruction: Covers elastic analysis of indeterminate structures, using the finite element method. Provides an introduction to fracture mechanics and the analysis and design of composite materials. Lecture, discussion, and problem solving are employed.

  Credit Recommendation: In the upper division baccalaureate category, 2 semester hours in structural engineering.

More recently, ACE has extended into other fields this way of assessing the learning accomplished by adults outside the formal education system and of relating it to formal study programmes. In the Armed Forces, quite apart from the wide range of courses which can be undertaken voluntarily and the course requirements in general fields, there are Occupational Specialities: requirements in specific skills which have to be met before a particular rank can be reached or military tasks assigned. The evaluation systems used for these internal purposes are highly developed and include written and practical tests. This system is also being used with apprenticeship training and this is, incidentally, a clear indication of the way the two worlds of formal education and of employment are coming together perforce. Some of the equipment installed by production industry and used for laboratory work in its employee training is far more expensive and extensive than most colleges can afford. Yet colleges are supposed to be training the future employees for those very establishments. ACE evaluators have been so impressed with the equipment used for training apprentices and with the range of skills and knowledge which they are required to master that they plan to publish a manual to help colleges make their own assessments of local apprenticeship courses for credit awards, just as for existing recognition of noncollegiate study. The examples which follow (figures 3 and 4) show the implications clearly. What is particularly significant about the apprenticeship scheme is that the feasibility study was conducted by a government department – the Department of Labor.

Figure 3: An 'Army-Enlisted Military Occupational Speciality Exhibit' with credit recommendations, from the *Guide to the Evaluation of Educational Experiences in the Armed Forces.*

Field Radio Repairman
   31E20, 31E40
   Exhibit Dates: 10/73–Present.

Career Management Field: 31 (Field and Area Communications Maintenance), *subfield* 312 (Tactical Electronics Maintenance).

Description:

Summary: Inspects, tests, and performs maintenance on FM radios, single side band radios, and radio teletypwriter equipment.

Skill Level 20: Performs testing and maintenance procedures; dismantles components, traces continuity, locates malfunctioning parts, and repairs faulty circuitry parts; uses multimeters, oscilloscopes, signal generators, and other equipment to locate and repair malfunctioning circuits; computes voltage, current, resistance, and power using Ohm's Law and Watt's Law functions.

Skill Level 40: Able to perform the duties required for Skill Level 20; supervises field radio equipment maintenance programs and instructs in maintenance procedures and techniques; diagnoses and determines causes of unusual and complex cases of equipment malfunction or nonfunction; interprets complex circuit and schematic diagrams; requisitions supplies; prepares, reviews, and consolidates technical and administrative reports; normally supervises 8–15 persons.

Note: May have progressed to 31E40 from 31E20, 31B20, or 32B30 (Field Communications Electronic Equipment Mechanic).

Recommendation, Skill Level 20: In the vocational certificate category, 3 semester hours in basic electricity (DC), 3 in basic electronics (AC), 3 in communications electronics, and 3 in electronic components (solid-state and vacuum tubes), for a total of 12 semester hours. In the lower-division baccalaureate/associate degree category, 3 semester hours in basic electricity (DC), 3 in basic electronics (AC), 3 in communications electronics, and 2 in electronic devices (solid-state and vacuum tubes), for a total of 11 semester hours. Advanced standing in a radio-television repairman

fraction, and absorption; knows the method for controlling light and illumination; knows the nomenclature of lenses, lens construction, and the meaning and relationship of focal length, aperture, and image formation, including enlargements and reductions; knows types of copy; knows the chemical properties, characteristics, and reactions of the various processing solutions (developers, stopbaths, fixers, etc.) used in the graphic arts photographic industry; knows the physical properties, different bases, dimensional stability, photographic characteristics, speed, color sensitivity, and the reaction to filtered light of various photographic films and papers; differentiates between line, continuous tone, and color copy in graphic arts photomechanics; determines various types of line copy and photographs each type, using process cameras, contact methods, and enlargers; knows the graphic arts industry methods for making halftones (glass screens, contact screens, and prescreened film); knows methods for controlling tonal ranges with both mechanical (gray scales) and electronic (densitometers) devices; makes halftones, using each of the various methods; knows and uses methods requiring special-effect contact screens, dropout halftones, duotones, and positive screened prints and positives.

Second Year: Knows theories and techniques of color separation photography; applies additive and subtactive color theory; applies direct, indirect, and scanning methods in producing sets of separation negatives; is knowledgeable about sensitometry and densitometry; uses technical equipment to measure optical density and to plot density ranges; uses several masking techniques for color correction, including single-stage masking, two-stage masking, camera-back masking, Ektacolor masks, Agfa-Gevaert multi-masks, and Kodak's tri-masks; produces separation negatives by using the enlarger, contact, and process camera methods; determines method of masking for each set of separation negatives; screens sets of separation negatives (either positive or negative form) by enlarger, contact, and process camera methods; uses several methods of pre-press proofing for each set of separations.

Third Year: Applies knowledge and skills in the performance of a variety of progressively more complex on-the-job tasks.

Fourth Year: Applies knowledge and skills in the performance of a variety of still more complex on-the-job tasks. Has completed the requirements for journeyman certification.

Recommendation, First Year: In the lower-division baccalaureate/associate degree category, 2 semester hours in halftone photography and special effects, 2 in a practicum in graphic arts, 1 in photographic chemistry, and 1 in light and optics, for a total of 6 semester hours.

Recommendation, Second Year: In the lower-division baccalaureate/associate degree category, 4 semester hours in a practicum in graphic arts, 2 in halftone photography, 1 in photographic chemistry, 1 in light and optics, 1 in theory of color separation photography and control devices, 1 in masking techniques, 1 in separation negatives, and 1 in screening and proofing, for a total of 12 semester hours.

Recommendation, Third Year: In the lower-division baccalaureate/associate degree category, 8 semester hours in a practicum in graphic arts, 2 in halftone photography, 1 in photographic chemistry, 1 in light and optics, 1 in theory of color separation photography and control devices, 1 in masking techniques, 1 in separation negatives, and 1 in screening and proofing, for a total of 16 semester hour

Recommendation, Fourth Year: In the lower-division baccalaureate/associate degree category, 12 semester hours in a practicum in graphic arts, 2 in halftone photography, 1 in photographic chemistry, 1 in light and optics, 1 in theory of color separation photography and control devices, 1 in masking techniques, 1 in separation negatives, and 1 in screening and proofing, for a total of 20 semester hours.

Electrician Apprentice (Inside)

Length of Program: Four Years.

Evaluation Site: International Brotherhood of Electrical Workers Local 441 and National Electrical Contractors Association Joint School, Tancho Santiago Community College District, Santa Ana Junior College, Santa Ana, Orange County, California. Job sites in Orange County, CA.

Exhibit Dates: 1971–Present.

Program Objective: To educate and train apprentices for journeyman status in the electrical construction (inside) industry.

Description:

First Year: Knows the principles of direct current, alternating current, and electro-magnetism; knows the National Electrical Code requirements pertaining to cable conduit and grounding and applies them; knows how electric motors operate; knows and understands Ohm's Law, series circuits, parallel circuits, magnetism, and motors; knows safety procedures and first aid resuscitation; reads and sketches evaluation views and plot plans and understands the symbols and scales used; knows materials used in the electrical construction industry, including residential, commercial, and industrial, such as wires and composition, cables, conduit, conductors, insulation, joints, fasteners, and fuses; under supervision, installs electrical apparatus such as cables, conduit, tubing, outlet boxes, outlets, fixtures, and securing and holding devices at various job sites; receives orientation on the apprenticeship form of education and training, the electrical industry, the history of the electrical industry, the International Brotherhood of Electrical Workers, local union by-laws, and the history of the operation and contribution of the National Electrical Contractors Association.

Second Year: Knows electrical meters and instruments and how to install and use them; knows transformer types, classifications, construction, singlephase connections and diagrams; knows the National Electrical Code requirements relating to grounding, grounded conductors, and calculations for service, feeders, and branch circuits of residential and small commercial installations. Knows sketching of mechanical parts; uses algebra and trigonometry in making calculations for AC circuits with various configurations of inductance, capacitance, and resistance; has ability to bend small conduit sizes in bends, offsets, kicks, and saddles; knows the operating principles of refrigeration and air conditioning systems and common troubles in these systems; knows the elements of rigging; knows electric motor mechanical drive and load connections; knows operating principles and connections for incandescent lamps and fire alarms; uses architects' blueprints and layouts; knows first aid procedures, including those for electric shock victims; knows safety rules and practices for the electric construction industry; knows the rudiments of parliamentary procedure; performs increasingly complex work tasks through a series of six-month job rotations.

Third Year: Knows and applies National Electrical Code requirements for capacitors, electric motors, and hazardous locations, including Class I, II, and III installations; uses blueprints of multi-floor structures for structural details, floor plans, service entrances, and distribution, risers, and general circuiting; knows additional details of alternating current, including power factor correction, three-phase circuits and motors, and fluorescent lamps and ballasts; knows bending of intermediate size conduit, including use of hydraulic benders; knows theory of operation, connection, and control of electric motors, including split phase, capacitor, repulsion, shaded-pole, and universal type; knows three-phase transformer connections; knows how to analyze and repair malfunctions in motor control; knows motor protective devices; applies knowledge by assuming increasingly complex responsibilities and performing complex tasks in work settings that are rotated each six months.

Fourth Year: Knows National Electrical Code requirements pertaining to wire closets, junction boxes, and stairway and emergency lighting and applies them; makes metric system conversions; understands and applies rules pertaining to radiation exposure, protection, reaction, and other features of nuclear safety; knows transistor principles and circuits and vacuum tube fundamentals; uses electronic testing equipment; understands basic rectifier circuits, amplifier circuits, special circuit applications, and transistor utilization; understands static control fundamentals, including concepts, circuits, analysis and applications; knows and understands motor maintenance; understands and applies alternating current applications in industrial electricity; understands the fundamentals of temperature, pressure, and flow; understands instrumentation systems; installs and tests electrical construction materials; uses electrical construction equipment.

Recommendation, First Year: In the lower-division baccalaureate/associate degree category, 2 semester hours in basic electricity, 1 in National Electrical Code, 1 in blueprint reading and sketching, 1 in orientation to electrical construction, 1 in electrical construction materials and methods, and 1 in field experience in electrical construction, for a total of 7 semester hours. Also recommend one-third of requirements toward a Vocational Certificate in Electrical Trades of 7 semester hours.

Recommendation, Second Year: In the lower-division baccalaureate/associate degree category, 4 semester hours in basic electricity, 3 in electrical construction materials and methods, 2 in field experience in electrical construction, 2 in National Electrical Code, 2 in technical mathematics, 2 in blueprint reading and sketching, 1 in orientation to electrical construction, 1 in safety and first aid, and 1 in shop practices, for a total of 18 semester hours. Also recommend two-thirds of requirements toward a Vocational Certificate in Electrical Trades or 18 semester hours.

Recommendation, Third Year: In the lower-division baccalaureate/associate degree category, 4 semester hours in basic electricity, 4 in electrical construction materials and methods, 1 in National Electrical Code, 1 in blueprint reading and sketching, 3 in field experience in electrical construction, 2 in technical mathematics, 2 in industrial electricity, 1 in motor controls, 1 in orientation to electrical construction, 1 in safety and first aid, and 1 in shop practices, for a total of 21 semester hours. Recommend that a Vocational Certificate in Electrical Trades be awarded at the successful completion of the third year of the program.

Recommendation, Fourth Year: In the lower-division baccalaureate/associate degree category, 5 semester hours in electrical construction materials and methods, 4 in basic electricity, 4 in National Electrical Code, 4 in blueprint reading and sketching, 4 in field experience in electrical construction, 3 in industrial electricity, 2 in safety and first aid, 2 in motor controls, 1 in motor maintenance, 2 in technical mathematics, 2 in shop practices, 2 in electronics, 1 in instrumentation, and 1 in orientation to electrical construction, for a total of 37 semester hours.

Given the number of individuals and organizations who are brought into a working relationship by it, this syllabus review procedure is of inestimable significance. The central feature is that it is based on documentary evidence which can be checked and assessed on its own terms, so that academic evaluators can move with assurance in fields where they are acknowledged experts. The terms of reference are clear. The rules of academic procedures can be followed. Judgements are explicit.

ACE's work is merely the latest example of a policy which dates back to 1918 and the end of World War I. Then ACE evolved a plan for awarding specified numbers of credits on account of years of war service. (After World War II, in a similar way, in Britain ex-service men and women were permitted to graduate after a shortened course of study, on account of the period of service they had completed when in normal times they would have been studying in a university or college.) It was to cope with the returning numbers of service personnel after World War II, which it was anticipated would seek to enroll for higher education, that ACE developed the system which has been described.

Simultaneously ACE has been associated with the use of examinations for adults as means of academic claims for credits towards graduation in the baccalaureate degree. General Educational Development tests are now available throughout the country leading to diplomas equivalent to high school diplomas. The College Entry Examinations Board introduced its College Level Examination Programme (CLEP) in 1966 with support from the Carnegie Foundation. There are now fifty of these examinations covering a wide range of subjects taken each year by over 140,000 candidates. More than 1500 colleges, ranging from two-year Community Colleges to Ivy League Institutions, use the results of these examinations as part of their entry assessment and placement procedures. ACE has evaluated syllabuses and publishes a set of precise recommendations of the credits which can properly be awarded according to the examination scores achieved.

CLEP works as a national external examination system for adults. Syllabuses are published with recommended reading and indications about the kind of examination which will be set. Timetables are published with lists of examination centres. The names of colleges and universities which recognize CLEP examinations are also available. So adults everywhere have the opportunity, first of trying themselves out for higher education study without any necessary commitment, and then of working at undergraduate studies for interest while knowing that the credit they can win will be accepted if and when they choose to follow their studies in a college or university, provided that it accepts CLEP results.

The system works on a customer payment basis. The first examination entry costs $22 and each additional entry another

$18, provided they all fall within the same month. Institutions pay $20 for each of ACE's two evaluation reports on courses. Individuals pay for textbooks, courses and examinations, and their fees to the university or college. Institutions charge for any credits which may be granted as if they were students following regular classes. Fees are calculated according to the number of credits a course carries: the more credits, the higher the fees. Although most of the candidates are younger college entrants and the examinations are not designed specifically for adults, the CLEP registration *Guide*[1] is clearly written with adults in mind: 'On the job experience, purposeful reading, adult school or correspondence courses, or television or taped courses, may have prepared you to earn college credit . . . People of all ages interested in pursuing a college education have reduced costs in time and money by successfully completing CLEP tests.'

With the powerful backing of the American Council of Education these approaches for enabling adults to find their way into higher education, making use of what they have learnt beforehand, present no great difficulties where academic and administrative staff accept them as part of their institution's policies. This development is based on the scrutiny of existing syllabuses supplemented by site visits and consideration of attainment levels of existing formal systems of instruction which are not the responsibility of higher education, but which may lead to degree level work.

Field work is the other development of off-campus work; it also is based on the principle that baccalaureate standards can be reached without being formally taught in a college or university. But there the resemblance ends; field work encourages all forms of life and work experience which provide opportunities for experiential learning – learning by doing. With field work or experiential learning there can be no detailed syllabuses to be evaluated by a central team of eminent academics to produce a national definition of standards. The requirements for assessing field work for credit in the baccalaureate

[1] New York: College Entrance Examination Board.

degree are bound to be quite different.

Field work provides opportunities for experiential learning, such is the term used to describe what is learned from work and life experience. Obviously, experiential learning includes learning from the practical experience provided in some co-op courses (sandwich courses in Britain). More significantly, it includes any learning that can be assessed academically, whatever its source. A student attached to a Housing Agency could be learning about the legal position of tenants and landlords, social security payments to individuals, the social dynamics of voluntary agencies and their clients, and business and office management. An internship with a newspaper or television station could provide opportunities for learning about journalism or programme production, as well as the day to day technical and management issues for the media. A period spent in a politician's office can offer ways of learning about the machinery of government, the development of policy as well as the nature of a contemporary political party. The possibilities of learning from different forms of field work and experience are limitless, and all are comprehended by the generic tag, experiential learning.

Co-op courses alone are responsible for a rapid extension of the practice of experiential learning. The practice of arranging alternating periods of classroom tuition and practical experience has gone far beyond the conventional sandwich courses in engineering, social work, teaching and the professions. In some institutions all degree programmes in the liberal arts are organized as co-op courses. In others it is an option. The increase in numbers of students involved in the US is striking. In 1970 there were some 30,000 students on co-op courses; by 1978 the estimate was some 170,000.

Service learning is another source of experiential learning and it has seen an equally dramatic increase. In this, a student works in voluntary public service and at the same time is engaged on some specific learning assignments. It might be in community work, in housing, in financial or legal aid in educational provision. By 1976 there were more than 1000 officially organized schemes of this kind in higher education institutions throughout the USA. Overseas educational programmes have been another growth area for experiential learning. By 1978 the Council on International Educational Exchange estimated that there were about 25,000 American undergraduates studying overseas, as part of their higher education programmes and many of these offered experiential learning opportunities.

In the winter of 1977 the first national survey was conducted of the kinds of experiential learning which were being undertaken by degree students. The Council for the Advancement of Experiential Learning undertook the work with the co-operation of the Educational Training Service and the support of the Kellogg Foundation. The categories used were these:

- *Career Exploration:* Supervised placement in business, government, a service organization, or a profession in order to analyze career possibilities and to develop employment-related skills.
- *Career or Occupational Development:* Placement chosen by student, in consultation with an adviser, to provide advancement in skills and experience related to a specific career.
- *Co-operative Education:* Classroom experience integrated with practical work experience in industrial business, government, or service organizations in the community. The placement is an essential element in the educative process in that some minimum amount of work experience and minimum standard of successful performance on the job are included in the requirements of the institution's degree.
- *Preprofessional Training:* Service in assigned responsibilities under the supervision of a professional in education, medicine, law, social work, nursing, or the ministry, in order to apply the theories and knowledge learned in the classroom.
- *Public Service Internship:* Service in an appropriate institu-

tion for a specific period of time, usually ten to fifteen weeks.

- *Social or Political Action through Service Learning Internship:* Placement, under faculty sponsorship, that provides an opportunity for students to work for change, either through community organizing, political activity, or research/action projects.
- *Personal Growth and Development:* A programme in an off-campus setting that is designed to further personal growth and development, such as the wilderness survival programs, apprenticeship to an artist or craftsman, or participation in an established group psychological or human relations programme.
- *Field Research:* An independent or group research project in the field, supervised by a faculty member, in which the concepts and methods of an academic discipline such as geology, archeology, geography or sociology are applied.[1]

So far no reference has been made to the experiential learning acquired by adults before they enroll in higher education. Just as ACE's pioneering efforts have brought so much informal adult learning within formal academic recognition, so adults' experiential learning has come to be recognized in the same way as that of undergraduates on, say, service learning or overseas programmes.

This development has been rapid, extensive and even, to some of its most convinced supporters, profoundly worrying. Their concern was about standards. As a direct result of the Commission on Non-Traditional Study in 1973, the Carnegie Foundation funded the Cooperative Assessment of Experiential Learning, (CAEL), which began work in 1974. Subsequently CAEL received additional financial help from the Ford Foundation, the Lilly Endowment, and the Fund for the

---

[1] Joan Knapp and Leta Davis, 'Scope and Varieties of Experiential Learning' in *New Directions for Experiential Learning*, 1, 1978, edited by Morris T. Keeton and Pamela J. Tate, San Francisco: Jossey-Bass.

Improvement of Postsecondary Education. CAEL began as a group of ten institutions of higher education, eight universities and two community colleges who agreed to work together with the Educational Testing Service in the assessment project. 'The purpose of the project is to develop procedures and material that will be useful in strengthening the assessment of experiential learning in higher education,' declared the CAEL validation report which was published in December 1976 as the summary of the project. By that time there were some two hundred institutions working with the CAEL project, which gives some indication of the extent of the concern about assessment and academic standards in relation to experiential learning, and the willingness of institutions to commit themselves to the search for acceptable procedures. This is not altogether surprising, since from the publication of the report of the Commission on Non-Traditional Study, it had been widely recognized that the assessment of experiential learning needed to be improved.

Assessing experiential learning is a complex business. Again, to quote from CAEL's validation report, 'For several reasons the assessment problem is more complicated than is true in the case of classroom learning; experiential learning tends to be highly individualistic; by its nature the potential range of relevant learning experiences is broad and not well defined; and experiential learning is often not subject to close faculty supervision. Thus, the need for sound new methods of assessment is associated with such familiar problems as establishing credibility of programmes, minimizing the abuse of flexible credit policies, and insuring public recognition of credit granted. At the same time there is the equally important problem of improving the value of assessment to the individual.'

CAEL began its task by selecting four priority areas. Noting that there are various types of competence, different contexts for learning, alternative methods of assessment, and different parties to the assessment, CAEL chose one important instance of each:

- *Assessing the Achievement of Interpersonal Skills* (an important competence): Experiential learning frequently involves application of knowledge in situations that depend upon interpersonal skills and offer special advantages for developing such competences.
- *Use of Portfolios in Assessing Non-Sponsored Learning* (an important method): Assessment of non-sponsored learning most often begins with preparation of a portfolio which presents pertinent information and documentation, and this process is of special current interest to many institutions.
- *Assessing the Learning Outcomes of Work Experience* (an important arena): The relation of education to work has attained national significance, and the various types of 'work' experience are among the most common forms of experiential learning offered for assessment.
- *Use of Expert Judgement in Assessing Learning Outcomes* (an important assessor): Much experiential learning is highly individualized, based on unique combinations of experience, and must necessarily be assessed through some form of expert judgement rather than objective instruments.

From the beginning, CAEL produced a series of reports which gave the collaborating institutions the kinds of information and stimulus (which had been lacking beforehand) for working out the procedures best suited to their own circumstances. In 1977, the Cooperative Assessment of Experiential Learning became the Council for the Advancement of Experiential Learning. As the initial project came to an end, the participating institutions decided that their collaboration was too important for the future of higher education in the USA to be allowed to lapse. Further funding from the Kellogg Foundation enabled it to move into a new phase of work concentrating on the institutional changes which were necessary in the adoption of experiential learning programmes. By 1981 CAEL has some 350 associated institutions, has provided 30,000 training days for faculty staff in training programmes during 1977–80, and is being used by government and state bodies as a consultant in the field.

Throughout this work under the leadership of Morris Keeton, formerly Provost of Antioch College and now President of CAEL, this has been the reference point: 'Experiential learning refers to learning in which the learner is directly in touch with the realities being studied. It is contrasted with learning in which the learner only reads about, hears about, talks about, or writes about these realities but never comes into contact with them as part of the learning process.' Put another way, experiential learning typically involves not merely observing the phenomenon being studied but also doing something with it.

For convenience CAEL differentiates between two categories of experiential learning: sponsored and non-sponsored. 'We speak of experiential learning activity as "sponsored" here if and only if it occurs in the context of an institution of higher education where the learner is officially registered and the activity an accepted part of the student's programme of studies. Failing to meet any element of this set of conditions, the experiential learning activity is "non-sponsored".'[1] This distinction is particularly important, for almost by definition most adults seeking credit for what they know at entry to higher education are asking for recognition of non-sponsored experiential learning. To assess what an adult claims to know on the basis of the life and work experience means being prepared to bring in a wide range of factors, far wider than is customarily used in formal examinations. The implications of this kind of undertaking are far-reaching. Hence the second period of CAEL activities is concerned explicitly with questions of institutional development and change, and it is here that the assessment of non-sponsored experiential learning is of profound importance for the theory and practice of experiential learning as a whole.

[1] *New Directions for Experiential Learning*, 1, 1978, San Francisco: Jossey-Bass.

Adult learning acquired as non-sponsored learning of course involves no tutorial or academic supervision. If credit towards a degree is to be given, valid and reliable assessment procedures must be able to demonstrate that the learning is the equivalent to collegiate learning and open to public scrutiny. Assessments must not only examine the content of the learning at a superficial level but also the ability to apply the learning in analysis and synthesis as an indication of the conceptual level of understanding. Without a syllabus to consider, the inquiry has to elucidate what it is that a person claims to know, the validity of that claim and whether this knowledge could be related to college work. This acts as a powerful correction to the less rigorous approach which has sometimes been adopted for the assessment of sponsored experiential learning. 'Signing off' is the term used for acceptance by a member of staff that a period of work experience has been completed satisfactorily. If the signing off is based on nothing more than a report from the work place to the effect that the student has completed his period satisfactorily, it is merely accepting the completion of the experience as a proper basis for awarding academic credit. Even a report written by the student may go little beyond that. It was just these kinds of practices which led to the anxieties described earlier; experience, which may be very valuable in itself, should not be confused with learning which can be certificated. So adults and the learning they claim to have acquired outside formal educational institutions are bringing very important influences to bear on the issue of the academic standards obtained from experiential learning. They are doing this because the principles on which the assessment of experiential learning is made are similar, if not identical, whether sponsored or non-sponsored. CAEL's summary statement of these principles in Warren Willingham's *Principles of Good Practice in Assessing Experiential Learning*[1] makes this clear (figure 5).

'Portfolio Assessment' is the term commonly used for con-

[1] Columbia, Md.: CAEL, 1977.

Figure 5: Six basic steps in assessing experiential learning – their order and application to prior and sponsored learning.

Step	Prior Learning	Sponsored Learning
IDENTIFY	1. Identify college-level learning acquired through life experience	2. Set specific learning objectives that fit the goals and the learning site
ARTICULATE	2. Show how and what parts of that learning are related to the degree objective	1. Decide on general learning goals that are related to the degree objective
DOCUMENT	3. Verify or provide evidence of learning	4. Maintain an integrated record as evidence of learning
MEASURE	4. Determine the extent and character of learning acquired	5. Determine whether learning meets the criterion standard previously set
EVALUATE	5. Decide whether the learning meets an acceptable standard and determine its credit equivalence	3. Determine the appropriate criterion standard required for credit
TRANSCRIBE	6. Record the credit or recognition of learning	6. Record the credit or recognition of learning

ducting a systematic investigation of what an adult claims to know under the general heading of nonsponsored learning. Evidently the phrase is borrowed from the graphic arts: a collection of items showing the best work. Empire State College of the State University of New York has a highly developed system. Experts make judgements on the quality and quantity of a student's knowledge within a defined field of a discipline, and relate the level of that knowledge to the different years of a typical four-year degree. Examples of two such evaluations, as they are called, follow (figures 6 and 7).

Figure 6: Example of an evaluation of experiential learning in political science.

To: Assessment Committee   Date: December 20
From: Evaluator
Subject: Student's Advanced Standing

On December 14, the student spent the day here where he answered sets of questions designed to allow him to display his knowledge of American governmental structures, operations, and the political process.

The assessment session was divided into time spent preparing written responses to my questions and to time spent discussing the student's answers. The student was able to answer most questions and prepared approximately 10 pages of single-spaced, typed material for my examination. I read and discussed that material with the student.

In the paragraphs which follow, I have described the student's responses and made credit recommendations. At the end of this report there is a summary and a set of learning components that I feel should be entered in his degree program in place of the current material.

1. American National Government

I believe the student has a working knowledge of the basic structure and functions of our national government. He was able to describe the main elements in national government. I would compare his knowledge to that gained from taking a lower division, 3 semester-hour course at the Community College level.

The student knows the way the House of Representatives operates and can describe its size, composition, and basic organization. He is also familiar with reform proposals such as the effort to extend periods in office from the current two years to four years. He can discuss the reasons for the current system of rather frequent elections and can describe the problems created by the need to stand for election every two years. The student was able to describe the Senate in a similar manner and was also generally familiar with its structure, and so on.

The student was able to develop a basic description of the Presidency and the executive branch of government. His knowledge of the Supreme Court was less solid and he had difficulty organizing information about important decisions.

I asked him to speak about the national political parties and their respective factions. He was able to describe regional political preferences and to explain their origin. For example, he knew that the South's experience in the Civil War and Reconstruction was important to any explanation of its preference for the Democratic Party.

2. Local Government in New York State

This is one of the student's strongest areas. In addition to being familiar with local government's operations in a particular region, the student is also able to discuss general issues. For example, he can describe the strengths and weaknesses of the partisan form of local government and the nonpartisan system. He makes the standard observations about the nonpartisan system's tendency to conceal real political loyalties and alliances as well as to make it difficult for voters to know each candidate's allegiances. He was able to give specific examples of each form of government and to illustrate its strengths and weaknesses. (He noted that the partisan form tends to increase the importance of political organizations and to make it possible to increase political accountability. He also noted that when one party dominates and has a strong machine that the advantages of the partisan system are diminished in as much as it becomes difficult to mount an effective opposition to the governing party.)

He was able to make similarly sophisticated observations about local interest groups and how they operate.

As one who has observed local politics for fourteen years, the student has a rich knowledge of how parties collect money, organize support, respond to various pressures, and so on. If an Empire State College student were to try to gain an equivalent amount of learning through the contract process, it would take him many months of intensive study and field work. Therefore, I have no difficulty recommending 8 credits advanced standing for this learning. In fact, I think 8 credits is a very, very small award for this.

3. New York State Government

This is a very strong area. The student knows much more about the operations, structures, and politics of State government than the several students I know who have completed five-month internships in Albany with the legislature.

The student can describe partisan voting patterns and their roots in regional needs and differences. He is also familiar with the ways in which various compromises are made when support is needed from the 'other' side of the aisle. He has a detailed knowledge of the operations of the committee systems. He knows who occupies the most important offices in each party and how they relate to the executive office as well as to local political structures.

The representation of individual interests, group interests, community interests, and so on is something which the student can discuss and illustrate with reference to actual issues such as the dairy industry. He could explain how individual farmers find it impossible to communicate their needs and therefore have to organize a lobby; how the lobby then takes on certain responsibilities for the group and may obscure the needs of particular individuals, and so on.

The student very effectively illustrated the problems of representation. That is to say, he wrote and spoke about group interests versus individual interests; the community versus the lobby; the regions versus the State.

The student also knows the proportional representation system and the way districts are created, especially in his region.

It is indeed difficult to recommend a specific amount of credits for the student's knowledge of State government. I do know that it is clearly the type of learning that takes many years to achieve. Therefore, my recommendation, 13 credits, is conservative. If one of my students were to spend a full semester working as an intern and studying the politics of state government full time, I don't think he would reach the level of knowledge displayed by this student during the interview.

4. Comparative Political Structure: U.S. and Canada

The student can describe several basic differences between local government in the United States and local government in Canada. He pointed out that American cities suffer from their tendency to become politically isolated from the suburbs; he noted that in Canada cities can extend their authority into the suburbs (the annexation process; he described the American fractionalization of various law enforcement services and the Canadian system's more rational organization).

The student discussed in detail a set of international issues related to the Thousand Island area.

I recommend that four credits of advanced standing be granted for the student's work in this area. (It would probably take a student two months of full-time work to gain the same type of learning; however, in limiting the recommendation to four credits, I have taken cognizance of the fact that advanced standing is also recommended for American local government, which is one part of the process of comparison.)

5. Issues in Public Administration and Community Development

The student understands basic issues in public administration and community development and has followed the main issues related to state and federal participation in various programs and the way federal and state grants tend to affect local developmental priorities. He defined and illustrated the tendency to shape local planning to suit federal and state funding opportunities and regulations rather than to seek and find ways to respond to the full range of local needs and possible solutions to local problems.

I recommend an additional four credits for this area of learning in order to recognize it as a rather special field which would require a month of research and field study to gain these insights.

Summary

I recommend the following award:

American Governmental Structures, Operations, and the Political Procell

1. American National Government   3 credits
2. N.Y. Local Government   8 credits
3. N.Y. State Government   3 credits
4. Comparative Government: Local and Regional Government in the U.S. and Canada   4 credits
5. Issues in Public Administration and Community Development   4 credits

The total recommendation is thirty-two credits. This is based on my view that the student's fourteen years of active observation of the political scene in the region and the State has resulted in learning that is far richer than that which would emerge from a typical one-year political internship.

The learning is very focused and detailed. It is not the same as one would expect from a political science major because it lacks the self-consciously evident theoretical knowledge that would have emerged from an academically oriented program of study.

I believe the learning is college level. It is of a different type than that which comes from the classroom and book-reading system. It is rich and deep and makes sense given the student's interest in careers in broadcasting and community service and development.

In speaking with the student, I discovered that he seems to have specialized knowledge of community fund raising. This should be investigated. It is possible that his skill and learning in this area have been underestimated.

What emerged in the many hours we spent talking about his learning and his future plans is a picture a little different from that shown in his degree program. In addition to broadcasting, there is a strong human and community service element in his degree program. This is mainly in the area of community political development and how this is related to social needs, and similar considerations.

If you have any further questions, please contact me.

Figure 7: Evaluation of the portfolio of an
Empire State student

To: Assessment Committee   Date: January 10
From: Evaluator
Subject: Evaluation of the Student's project:
          Development of a Telemetry System
          for the SUNYA Accelerator

The student has indicated a request for 8 credits for the work he has done in the design and development of a telemetry system that will both control and monitor the Dynamitron nuclear accelerator at the State University of New York at Albany.

I was asked to evaluate his work so I visited him at

SUNY on the morning of December 20. He described his work in general, and the project in particular. It was clear to me that the student has a state-of-the-art knowledge in the field of electronics, both analog and digital.

It is customary at my college to grant credit for project work after submitting a written report on it. I asked the student to do this, that is, to write such a report, and on December 29 he presented me with that report. His report, even though it may not be in the field of expertise of the members of the Committee, should be reviewed by them.

The report is general in that, as I had directed, he avoids the details of the design and concentrates on the overall problem and his method of solution.

- He describes the accelerator itself and the problems of controlling it in a 5 million volt environment.
- He shows why a communication system using fiber optic links is necessary to provide both electric isolation and the information channels.
- He then describes in more detail how the analog information is converted to a serial digital signal for transmission as light pulses over a fiber optic link.

Finally, despite all the precautions taken, electric discharges do occur, and his system must be protected from sparking. All leads to the electronic circuitry are passed through a two-stage shield and suppression filter using metal-oxide vanistors, an r-f choke, and back-to-back zener diodes.

The work completed so far is easily worth 8 semester credits. The system is nearly assembled, and the installation and testing of it will probably be worth 8 additional credits.

In my twenty-nine years of teaching, I have supervised nearly fifty Master's theses, undergraduate projects, and independent studies. I rate the student's work near the top of all of them. I therefore recommend that he be granted 8 semester hours of credit in the area of electronic design.

In addition to being interviewed, the students also assemble a portfolio setting out what they claim to know, documenting how they consider they have acquired that knowledge, and giving names of those who can verify the claims. For adults not familiar with methods of study or inexperienced in setting down things clearly on paper, this is daunting, if they are left to themselves. But they are not. The production of a portfolio is usually the result of extensive consultation with tutorial staff from the institution making the assessment and may take a considerable time to complete. Its evolution and compilation is all part of the process of identifying and recording the knowledge claimed. Having to articulate it clearly on paper constitutes an important part of learning in its own right, requiring a conceptual rather than a descriptive and anecdotal grasp of the knowledge claimed.

An example of the approach to assessing sponsored experiential learning comes from the official course description of an Urban Affairs Supervised Field Work internship offered in Boston University. (An internship is a work assignment in a work place approved by the university or college.) 'This course provides students with first hand field experience in public and private institutions that deal with urban issues. By placing students in agencies with a specific job or task to perform the course allows students to test their interests in particular vocational areas. The seminar which accompanies the placement attempts to facilitate discussions of organizational theory, issues of work and professional practice and theories of social change.'

Before they begin, the students draw up a contract with the field supervisor in the agency where the work is to be done. The first part of this contract specifies the tasks to be performed by the student, the hours to be worked, the arrangements for regular meetings between student and supervisor, starting and finishing dates, and telephone numbers and addresses for consultations. The second part of the contract specifies what the student anticipates learning during the period of work. The contract is a means of trying to ensure that student, teaching staff and field supervisor all have a clear understanding of what the sponsored learning is intended to achieve, and so underwrites the university's academic responsibility in overseeing the study of its registered students. On the basis of reports which students are required to submit, contributions to seminars and reports from field supervisors, assessments are made. The course gives three credits and students have to have worked for at least fifteen hours a week for ten weeks and attended six seminars.

For adults a contract for learning, or learning plan, is very important. It can easily be that the motivation to study for a degree does fit neatly into the courses of study available. On the basis of what they know already, adults often have a clear vision of what it is they wish to learn. For these people a learning contract is the means of converting such an idea into academic study. After consultation which may change the vision in the light of the nature of some academic disciplines, both student and tutor have an agreed course which measures up to the requirements of the disciplines involved and to the overall degree requirements of the institution. Contracts are formally considered by the appropriate academic committees of the institution. Full documentary evidence of what has been achieved is submitted to an assessment committee, who determine the credit to be awarded. In many ways this is for sponsored learning what the portfolio is for the assessment of non-sponsored learning.

All these various possibilities can be used within one degree programme. For example, the non-collegiate course work, CLEP examinations and non-sponsored experiential learning all appear in the Empire State College degree given in figure 8. The baccalaureate degree requirements at Empire State College include:

- at least 128 credits in all
- no more than 96 credits in 'advanced standing' (credits awarded to entrants for prior conventional coursework or experiential learning)

- at least 45 credits in studies of upper-division levels
- at least 24 upper-division credits for the 'concentration' or major
- for the BA, at least 96 credits (75 per cent) in liberal studies (or at least 50 per cent in liberal studies for the BS, or at least 25 per cent in liberal studies for the Bachelor of Professional Studies)

Empire State College is a convenient example to use since its regulations neatly summarize the way these different developments can all be put to the service of potential students; many institutions throughout the USA have also undertaken similar programmes. One other institutional development has to be added to the picture: Community Colleges. These have been the fastest growing section of higher education over the last decade. They were introduced to offer two-year Associate Degrees amongst an extensive range of courses designed specifically for the needs of the surrounding community. Adults have been attracted to Community Colleges in large numbers encouraged by their accessibility and by the fact that they were deliberately setting out to serve those who were not already making use of the higher education institutions. For those who wish to transfer to an institution offering the four-year baccalaureate, an Associate Degree gives two years of credit, requiring only two further years of study.

Men and women who left high school without diplomas for college entrance, especially those from minority ethnic groups and from lower income families in urban areas, have been enabled through Community Colleges to use the achievements in their lives and work experience as sources of learning with the hope of gaining credits towards a degree. Correspondingly, Community Colleges have been a strong influence in the development of experiential learning as they have recruited increasing numbers of students through their own experiential learning programmes.

It is impossible to give a typology of institutions engaged in

Figure 8: An Empire State College Degree Programme

Some Degree Programme components may have been satisfied through assessment of prior college-level learning. Those components are listed first. The first section includes two parts: (A) CREDIT BASED ON TRANSCRIPTS from other accredited colleges and universities; (B) CREDIT BY EVALUATION of College-level learning from other sources. This is followed by a listing of (C) CONTRACT LEARNING studies completed through Empire State College learning contracts.

Source	Concentration	General learning	Credits
A TRANSCRIPTS			
Westchester Community College 1968–1973	Administration		3
	Organization		3
	Supervision		3
	Public Relations		3
	Human Relations		3
	Political Science		3
	Criminal Law		3
		English Composition & Literature I	3
		English Composition & Literature II	3
		Speech	3
		College Algebra	3
		Basic Physiology & Anatomy	3
		Principles of Investigation	3
		Psychology I	3
		Psychology II	3
		Abnormal Phsychology	3
		Psychology of Adjustment	3
		Adolescent Psychology	3
		Introduction to Criminology	3
		Police Science Seminar	3
		Sociology I	3
	Concentration 21		
	General Learning 48		

Sociology II   3
Social Problems   3

Total Transcript Credit   69

B CREDIT BY EVALUATION

Iona College
1974

Criminalistics and the Forensic Sciences   3

Harrison Police Dept.
1957–Present

Management   4
Public Personnel Management   4
Human Factors in Management   4
Personnel Psychology   4

Teaching Techniques   4
Oral Communication   4

Concentration 16
General Learning 11

Total Credit by Evaluation   27

TOTAL ADVANCED STANDING   96

C CONTRACT LEARNING

Principles of Law of Labor Relations   4
Public Administration   4
Municipal Government & Administration   4
Public Finance   4
Accounting for Public Sector   4
Degree Program Planning   4
Constitutional Law   4
Economics   4

Concentration 20
General Learning 12

Total Contract Learning   32

DEGREE PROGAM TOTAL   128

the assessment of experiential learning. There is a general
tendency for Community Colleges to be more energetic in developing it because they exist – as a principal part of their
brief – to serve adult learners. However, the four-year colleges
in state systems and the state universities are needing to take
more account of adult learners, although this was not necessarily an original aim. They are perforce looking to ways of tapping
experiential learning for recruitment.

Two other things can be said. You can find institutions
engaged in sponsored learning but not the assessment of non-
sponsored learning. It is less usual to find it the other way round
(assessing prior learning but not sponsored learning). Certainly
one finds that those responsible in institutions for these programmes believe in them on educational grounds, whereas the
administrators are interested for pragmatic financial reasons.

All these facilities serving to encourage adults to pursue
studies within higher education have to be set in the wider
context of a pronounced characteristic of the adult population of
the USA. Reviewing national surveys of adult learners, K.
Patricia Cross estimated that one in four of the adult American
population joins with others in some form of organized learning
each year.[1] Demography and technology are prompting these
developments and the significance for higher education is obvious. The academic developments outlined in this chapter are
merely the measure of the significance.

This account of the learning facilities available through colleges and universities in the USA demonstrates a deliberate
matching of higher education provision to constituencies of
possible students. Institutions have changed what they offer
and how they offer it. CAEL found that in 1980 there were 1000
institutions engaged in non-sponsored learning and at least
1100 in sponsored learning. As a sign of the times it is significant
that the number of institutions known to be engaged in non-
sponsored and sponsored experiential learning is very much

---

[1] *Lifelong Learning: Purposes and Priorities*. Columbia, Md.: CAEL, 1979.

greater than the membership of CAEL and the other national organizations working in this field.

It would be a mistake, however, to think that the USA has solved its higher education problems. It has not. Many colleges and universities have not adopted any of these approaches; many academic staff are strongly opposed to them. Since it is inherent in some of the measures that the professional role of staff must change, and consequently that the stance and even the purpose of institutions must also change, this is entirely understandable. The essential point is that it would appear that American academic staff and higher education institutions have the means at their disposal, if they wish to use them, for coming to terms with the demographic and technological factors which are altering the world in which they exist.

In sum, they amount to a substantial shift in the relationships between institutions of formal education and individuals as potential and actual students. But more than that they amount to a shift in the position of higher education as an institution within a society with all its means of production, distribution and consumption. The learner as an active consumer has left the dependent client way behind. The individual is recognized as someone who may well have learned more than has been formally attested. To that extent, the individual has been accepted as the term of reference for any subsequent learning. The individual is also recognized as having his other own particular circumstances of home and working life and as needing to determine for himself how best to accommodate study to his other preoccupations. Further the individual is seen to be someone who may have well found notions of what he or she wants to know, which, with appropriate academic support and guidance, can become an academically valid programme of studies.

The world of employment has also moved to a different relationship with higher education. In acquiring recognition for some of the courses it provides for its own employees, such a change has inevitably followed. At both ends of its training and professional development schemes there is dramatic evidence of this. At one end, the intentions of ACE to produce a manual of guidance concerning the academic standing of certain apprenticeship courses is an impressive commentary on the educational capacity of some firms and corporations. At the other end of the academic scale, it has to be noted that Rank Xerox, Arthur D. Little Inc and IBM offer studies to their employees at doctoral level and are licensed to award PhDs. (Indeed, 20 of the top 100 corporations in the USA are licensed to award degrees.)

This is simply one example of the changes which are occurring throughout modern technological societies. Almost everyone doing almost anything now needs to know more in order to do it adequately. In the USA higher education is responding to these kinds of developments. The financial implications are of considerable importance too. Both in America and in Great Britain the public perception of education has changed. The easy support in the relatively affluent 1960s and early 1970s has been replaced by a somewhat grudging acceptance of the financial burden through taxation on paying for the service. Money lurks behind the accountability movement which has swept through state legislatures and school boards, with its difficult and yet beguilingly simple propositions that teachers should be required to work to defined standards, and be held accountable for their performance in teaching. For higher education financed through the state systems, the general disillusionment with students, and then with recently qualified young people as employees, makes state legislators very sensitive to their electorate's resistance to taxes. Publicly-funded institutions are finding their budgets trimmed if not yet drastically reduced. Anything which looks like an economy gets a good hearing.

This is where experiential learning fits in. For an adult, the length of time spent in becoming qualified is the vital factor: all other things being equal, the shorter the better. So if the credit awarded for experiential learning makes an appreciable reduction in the time required for graduation, there is clear gain. The improvement in salary and promotion which often result from a further qualification will begin sooner. If the degree was taken with the intention of helping to change occupation, then that too can begin sooner. Experiential learning also makes an absolute reduction in the cost to the student. The charges levied for evaluation vary considerably: a few institutions charge the same as for a full course using the credit equivalence to justify the fees. But others charge at a much lower level, a quarter or less. Experiential learning can yield a given number of credits at a cost lower than courses which produced the same credit. Conversely there is another factor at work. If an adult knows he may be awarded credit for his experiential learning, and knows it will save time in becoming qualified, there is considerable encouragement to become a student. So every adult encouraged by experiential learning credit to enrol brings fees to an institution which it would not collect at all if these adults did not enroll.

For the institution, then, experiential learning is an income raiser as well as a recruitment inducement. If it recruits students who would not otherwise enroll or collects evaluation fees which otherwise would not be paid, then in absolute terms financially it is better off. This is an important argument with academic staff who may resist the introduction of experiential learning programmes on the grounds that credit for work completed outside the institution is merely emptying the classrooms of students they would otherwise be teaching inside the institutions. But a rational consideration suggests that on all counts the professional security of academic staff is best tended through helping the institution to increase its fee income from students whichever credit-awarding system provides the money. If an institution is able to show a more healthy balance sheet as a consequence of introducing experiential learning programmes, then its general position is strengthened for undertaking those other parts of its academic work which are likely to be most prized by many of its staff. Perhaps more importantly, as a result of increasing the service it offers the adult community, it is likely to get a better hearing when arguing its case for funds.

All these financial considerations throw into higher relief the importance of proper safeguards to ensure the maintenance of appropriate academic standards. The seductive dangers are obvious and do not need an extensive commentary. There is a sufficient number of frauds, of phoney institutions issuing phoney qualifications, for the point to be made. It is this side to the system which was one of the reasons for responsible academic leaders in the US taking the initiative for ensuring proper standards of assessment in experiential learning which led to the development of CAEL.

The main emphasis in this chapter has been on the development in the US of means of matching the provision of higher education to the conditions of adult life and simultaneously extending the service of higher education to its constituents and securing its own future. The case is made for the value of experiential learning for mature adults. There is just as strong a case to be made for younger students. Some of these developments obviously affect the traditional 18 to 20 year old in higher education: different modes of study, full-time, part-time and periodic study, and credit transfer. But one – the assessment of sponsored learning – is particularly important for them because of its curriculum opportunities. It is also important as a further example of the way American institutions are trying to match their provision to the world in which their students live.

Liberal education itself is not held in the highest esteem these days. Professional and vocational education often get a better hearing. Yet graduates from liberal education are precisely what employers, corporations and official agencies of all kinds often require. Everyone agrees that the prime need now is for graduate employees to be able to analyse unfamiliar problems, produce solutions and turn those solutions into practice. In other words trained minds are valuable if they are able to apply their training particularly in contexts where people are going to complicate everything. Yet generally speaking higher education does little to prepare its graduate for this kind of employment. This is not arguing for a new version of vocational training. Apart from anything else, the re-training which nearly everyone will be required to undergo in the course of a working career makes that kind of preparation essentially short-term and of limited value. Indeed it could be actively unhelpful, for too specific a preparation for employment may put on psychological blinkers, making it more difficult to adjust to changes which are almost certainly in store. What is required is a study programme deliberately designed to include two elements which are, more often than not, missing: self study and career education with opportunities to assess personal suitability as against various occupations.

This is where experiential learning – sponsored learning – can be so valuable. Periods of work experience during the baccalaureate for those undergraduates who want it can provide opportunities for probing those two elements. This is just what many a co-operative education programme in the USA is trying to do. They provide the opportunity for young people to assess themselves against the requirements that will be made of them in employment, discovering their strengths and weaknesses in a particular work setting. They also present opportunities for young people to assess those working requirements against the expectations they have of fulfilling their own lives. In each case it is a diagnostic exercise with a chance of fewer square pegs trying to fit into round holes.

In addition, work experience confronts undergraduates with the need to solve unfamiliar problems. They may be good at academic problems when they can take their time about it, or even under the pressure of a three-hour examination. At work, however they may have to analyze immediate issues, under the pressure of not wasting time and therefore money. This may seem a lowly version of the complex problems which are the daily preoccupation of the senior managers which they may subsequently become. But it is a start; one which too many leave until it is almost too late. When organized carefully it can provide opportunities for systematic study as an integral part of a degree course.

This connection between experiential learning and a liberal arts programme brings studies closer to the requirement of the younger students as they try to discern their future in a fast changing world. It strengthens the appeal of liberal arts programmes by taking those preoccupations seriously and trying to provide for them. It is another means of bringing a technological society into closer contact with its educational system.

Perhaps the strongest strand running through all these various responses of higher education to the world which supports it, is that every one of them offer to men and women who are intending to work, or who are already at work in industry or commerce or personnel services, opportunities of using experience of work as a source of learning. A technological society is being recognized for what it is; a place where learning occurs, sometimes in unexpected places.

Britain, too, is a technological society. Its social and educational structures may be different but the needs of individuals are strikingly similar. It is the responsiveness of institutions to society which is the critical factor.

5

Programmes for Tomorrow's Students

The next two chapters consider developments to the existing provision in Great Britain which will enable higher education to provide the service it owes to the society which supports it. All of these developments are necessary if, when the numbers of 18 year olds has declined after 1985, the universities and colleges are to attract sufficient numbers to preserve the present structure of higher education and enable it to develop its research role as a vital national resource. These chapters focus in turn on individuals as potential students, on institutions which can serve them and on the staff of these institutions. Separately and together these chapters rest on the four-point case that has been made in the first half of this book: that more higher education is required; that a wider variety of ways of studying is needed; that, whatever the source of an individual's knowledge and skills, they should be eligible for formal recognition; and that these developments should take place without lowering present academic standards and at no additional cost. The order of these chapters is important. By considering first additions to present arrangements from the point of view of individuals, the onus is placed on institutions to respond. They will not be able to unless their academic and administrative staff are prepared to carry out the changes which follow from making additions to academic programmes.

The Knowledge Revolution

The next two chapters are written specifically about Britain. Many of the developments have proved themselves in the USA, although, as was shown towards the end of the previous chapter, there is room for improvements there. Much of the discussion applies, however, to higher education in modern technological societies throughout the world, while it raises important questions for less developed countries. The problems of maintaining access and quality in a period of financial stringency are fundamental wherever higher education is provided. Throughout these chapters there are frequent references to experiential learning. This refers to learning which is acquired from any activity which is not formal tuition; it does not refer to the activity itself. With that distinction made it is important to add that the use of experiential learning can be only one of the possible solutions to some of the problems of higher education.

To turn, then, to the students, arrangements for entry to courses, for study and for curricula all need reconsideration if more people are to make more effective use of higher education. This may involve reconsidering levels of academic study and even categories of awards, perhaps including sub-degree work. It certainly means extending the use of the present exceptional admission procedures and establishing an additional route to matriculation parallel to the present reliance on formal qualifications. It may mean exempting certain categories of potential students from matriculation altogether. It means a large extension of the opportunities for part-time study. It means recognizing that knowledge and skills acquired without reference to academic institutions can take individuals to attainment levels comparable with those currently required for first degrees. It also means accepting that the content of an academic curriculum can properly include learning derived from life and work experience.

Eligibility and entry to college or university is where the search for a better match has to begin. It simply is not the case that the only people who are qualified by aptitude and performance are those with two or more passes at 'A' Level or are amongst those present entrants to degrees validated by the Council for National Academic Awards (CNAA) who are admitted without formal qualifications, or those admitted annually to universities through special admission procedures. The data in Chapter 2 stand as proof of that. The annual controversies about the 'A' Level go some way to confirm it. When the results are published, and anxious candidates who have failed to achieve the required grades for entry besiege universities and polytechnics and colleges, the validity of 'A' Level results for higher educational admission is questioned. It is not that the grades are adjusted in some obscure way to the detriment of the examinees, but rather that undue reliance is placed on the results. As a broad guide to attainment and as an indication of likely performance in the future they are undoubtedly of value, but the difference between a grade C and a grade D pass is only a mark or two, as is the difference between a grade a and a fail. Even when overall results are added up, so that it doesn't matter whether the nine points, say, required by a particular department come from three passes at C grade (each one counting three points), or from a B, a C and a D grade (B:4; D:2), provided that the score still comes to the nine required: this still doesn't deal with the fundamental difficulty. A few marks in one or two examinations at the age of 18 after twelve years of schooling seen in the perspective of a lifetime does not seem an appropriate way of determining a course of study for many 18 year olds until they are 21. It is on the borderline between pass and failure, as with the controversial 11-plus examination used for selection for the former secondary grammar and technical schools in the tripartite system, that these regulations are such a serious matter. It is those candidates who find opportunities restricted just when they ought to be widening to allow for the maximum development.

The first point, then, about access to higher education is that the present standard way of achieving formal matriculation requirements should be supplemented by others. This does not mean simply accepting equivalent qualifications such as the

Ordinary National Diploma or Foundation units of the Open University (usually recognized in place of 'A' Levels). It means, first, finding out what people may know irrespective of how they have acquired that knowledge; and, second, providing an anteroom to degree study as a proving ground for those who are determined to attempt it but appear to have little else to offer as evidence of their suitability.

This moves straight into the field of experiential learning; the learning acquired from 'doing' which is not certified. The term experiential learning may not fit easily into the vocabulary in Britain, but it is difficult to find an improvement. The first official use of the term, so far as I have discovered, is in connection with studies funded by the Department of Education and Science (DES). The Educational Credit Transfer Project, directed by Peter Toyne and based at Exeter University, came across the idea in its first stage of work as it became clear that some applicants for courses were asking if their experience could be taken into consideration instead of obtaining an entry qualification. The second stage of work was to investigate the establishment of an information service concerning the available credit transfer, and this was approved by the Committee of Vice-Chancellors and Principals of Universities. The terms of reference of this second stage instanced one of the matters to be investigated as, 'the way in which and the extent to which information on credit available for "experiential learning" might be requested by students' (Toyne had visited CAEL as part of his investigation). The second mention is in the title of a project report issued in December 1979 by the Further Education Curriculum Review and Development Unit in the DES: 'Active learning: a guide to current practices in experiential and participatory learning'. This project was concerned with the 16–19 year old age group but, while not related to higher education directly, did bring the term into the vocabulary.

The principle – though not the terminology – of experiential learning as a basis for admission to higher education is already accepted and embodied in practice in universities, polytechnics and colleges. The Committee of Vice-Chancellors and Principals and the Trades Union Congress have jointly published a pamphlet called 'Mature students, a brief guide to university entrance'. The section on getting advice about going to university (paragraph 2) contains the following: 'They [universities] have a special procedure for considering mature candidates without the usual qualifications and it is helpful if, when you write for information, you provide brief details of your age, work, experience and any relevant educational courses taken since leaving school . . . Universities need to be satisfied that all candidates have certain minimum attainments which will enable them to follow and complete a course of study. Relevant qualifications or experience you may have will be taken into account. You may also be asked to take a special test or provide written work as a guide to your ability.' Some universities are more willing to accept mature students without formal qualifications than others. Sussex and Lancaster universities have always made it clear that they have been anxious to consider mature students lacking conventional matriculation requirements and both developed schemes deliberately designed to that end. Oxford and Cambridge colleges can always find way of admitting candidates they want in the college; and, from time to time, any university special admission committee considers application papers based on general grounds of familiarity with a discipline and exceptional personal circumstances which have convinced an admission tutor that they fall within the institution's ordinances and statutes. But these cases are comparatively rare.

The CNAA's guidance to polytechnics and colleges for admission to degree courses accepts that a proportion of any year's entry may be admitted without formal matriculation requirements. In practice it rarely amounts to more than fifteen per cent. Although that provision is not based on an explicit principle relating to experiential learning, the implication is that admission can be properly allowed on the basis of the sum total of a person's knowledge and skills and readiness for further study, which is the result of his life and work experience.

No new principle is being introduced therefore in seeking to widen access routes to higher education; it is rather a development of what already happens. It can lead to unfamiliar kinds of work and that is discussed further in the next chapter. But from the viewpoint of the person who at present does not consider himself as an applicant because he doubts his chance of success, it appears as a radical and dramatic extension of the present admission arrangements. He will be able to approach higher education to discover his suitability for advanced study on his own terms, rather than on those laid down principally with other kinds of applicants in mind. This will boost his own confidence; it will certainly be of profound significance to higher education once the perceptions change of many who are sceptical about its appropriateness. Any such alteration of the perceptions of potential students is perhaps the most important issue for higher education institutions.

The other way of extending present entry arrangements is the ante-room. There is no inherent reason why anyone who wished to begin a higher education course should not be permitted to do so after suitable counselling, but with formal admission to degree study being delayed until the end of the first year. Since the logical consequence of 'late developers' means that any formal system will exclude some people wrongly, simply allowing those with strong enough motivation to take the risk of beginning and later being rejected increases opportunities for individuals while guarding academic standards.

Experiential learning and the ante-room both offer practical alternatives to the stock comment which so often discourages potential applicants without the requisite 'A' Levels: 'Go and pass some 'A' Levels and we'll be glad to consider you'. Neither is a substitute for the preparatory courses which are being developed in some colleges and polytechnics especially for ethnic minorities, nor for the Open College scheme established by a group of further education colleges in the north west and the University of Lancaster, which serves as a multi-purpose introductory course for adult students, nor for the flexi-study arrangements made between the National Extension College and some further education colleges. There is room for as many schemes as can be devised to encourage applications from sections of the population so far unconvinced that higher education has anything to offer them.

Extending the access is only the beginnings of an attempt to alter the perceptions: similar extensions must be made to the kinds of study available. Here experiential learning can be seen as a means of enriching the curriculum. Within the present academic requirements for first degrees taught in universities and other institutions, it is possible to see how the knowledge and skills which can be learned from various forms of work experience can be included. If degree courses did include areas of study which are closely related to the life and experience of the student, so that the 'learner is directly in touch with the realities being studied', the curriculum would be brought nearer to potential students in the same way that extending admission possibilities brings higher education closer. Institutions could then be doing what the Robbins Committee urged seventeen years ago: taking seriously 'a vast mass whose performance both at entry and higher education and beyond depends greatly on how they have lived and been taught beforehand'.

For the curriculum that is very general; it needs to be specific. All discussions of the curriculum within higher education, or anywhere else for that matter, begin on the basis of a necessary connection between the conditions for entry, and the courses of study. At present many 'A' Level courses lead directly into degree studies. One of the loudest objections raised to proposals to reform the sixth-form curriculum comes from higher education teachers claiming that any reduction in the content of courses at 'A' Level would mean that sixth formers would not subsequently be able to cope with their courses in higher education. Three-year degrees might need to be extended to four years to compensate for this. The connection between entry and course could not be more pointed.

The same principle of connecting between entry and courses of study can be applied to admission based on experiential learning. The applicants' courses of study should, in part, and if they so wish, present an opportunity for further study in those areas of knowledge where they are already judged proficient. This should not be obligatory, but available as an option. At present the full time 'A' Level entrant who wishes to study political science, and has followed history at school but has not made a systematic study of politics, usually has the option of continuing some history, while beginning new subjects such as philosophy and economics. Similarly, the entrant who is judged through the assessment of experiential learning to be well enough grounded in business management, or social science or engineering, to cope with degree studies, should have the opportunity of continuing studies in those areas as well as beginning courses in completely new subjects. The same should be true for men and women who have gained knowledge and skills from experience other than in paid employment. Many women make systematic studies of child care and nutrition as part of their domestic responsibilities to make the tasks more worthwhile to them and sometimes to counteract the drudgery. Many adults develop hobbies which take them systematically into the technicalities of solar heating or local history, geology or archeology. Others undertake a wide range of voluntary work from serving as an elected member in local government and sitting on community service committees, to supporting professionals in the social services, leading youth groups and working for the Samaritans. From all these activities volunteers may acquire knowledge which not only stands as an adequate entry qualification but also identifies the area of further study. However, this may not be quite as straightforward to put into practice as it seems. For the student it may well turn out that what he already knows does not fit neatly into the syllabuses written for and regularly taught to younger undergraduates.

His knowledge may extend in part over several courses and his chosen further study may not be met by attending those classes. If his further studies are to be an extension without wasteful repetition of what he already knows, then they may need planning on an individual basis for independent study. As was mentioned earlier, there are one or two institutions where independent study is a normal part of the curriculum, but it is not generally available. It should be: for it is a form of study which holds many attractions for students of all ages. But if entry through taking into account learning acquired through experience became customary, then provision for independent study should be introduced as a consequence. Independent study is understood here to mean studies authorized, supervised and assessed on the same academic terms as work within taught courses, as a formal element in a degree programme; an option within a degree programme or an entire programme in itself depending on what was academically appropriate.

The motivation of students who can capitalize on existing experience is strong. It is especially attractive to older part-time students where their studies may contribute directly to promotion because their greater understanding is of value to their employer, or to greater responsibilities in their voluntary work. The activity they follow yields material for further study in their degree. They have a sense of an institution recognizing the relatedness of their work and study and so find considerable gratification in knowing that one is directly helping the other. From the educational point of view, they use their work place for study, and are learning in a particularly effective mode: 'the learner is directly in touch with the realities being studied'. Studying more carefully what you are doing day by day, and gaining a further qualification for doing so, has a commonsense appeal as well as being rooted in sound educational principles. Older full-time students can make similar use of what they have learned from their experience, and gain correspondingly a sense of self esteem.

This is one way in which accepting the academic validity of

experiential learning can change the curriculum to appeal to potential students. Another is to develop the principle of alternating periods of study in taught courses with periods of work experience, and extend it to spheres of activity which at present do not commonly feature. Sandwich courses need to be seen as a mode of education, rather than a means of providing practical experience during the overall preparation for joining a profession. Courses for engineers, social workers, teachers, doctors and, more recently, lawyers, accountants and potential managers, are often arranged as sandwich courses with field placements as a requirement. But from the point of view of a potential student there is no logical reason why any field of activity should be excluded from this. The critical requirement is that the practical experience can yield learning which is related in some way, and ideally fully integrated, with the academic study. This does not mean every part of the academic course bears a direct relationship to the experience which the practical work is providing, or vice versa, but that some part of the course should bring the two together. This would be a significant development of the present sandwich courses. For example, a dozen students all following a non-vocational programme who are all either currently engaged in some form of social work, whether paid or voluntary, or wishing to gain some experience of social work having had little or none so far, could all study different subjects within their degree and yet share this interest in common. They would all be given field placements where what they were expected to contribute to and learn about social work was made explicit before the placement began. They would meet regularly at seminars to pool, analyse and evaluate their experience and learning. Practice and theory would be brought together. The same arrangements could be made for students in a non-vocational degree who were all interested in the tourist industry, in journalism whether in the press or radio or television), in the retail trade, or in commerce. In this way, the learning gained from work experience would be a recognized part of an academic course of study though it might be on a much smaller scale than is the case with the present sandwich courses. It would have considerable appeal, for a reason which has not been touched on so far.

One of the most difficult tensions to resolve within higher education arises from the differing intentions, expectations and perceptions of academic studies held by academic staff and students. Quite reasonably, most teachers base their professional expertise in their own chosen subject, and see their prime role as leading students towards their own level of mastery. This is not necessarily study for its own sake, though this is what many academics would dearly like to assert. It is teaching students to study to achieve some level of competence in the subject within its own requirements, whether there is any further purpose in it or not. In the process, some students may become competent in solving problems – transferability, where the mind trained through systematic study may have a general competence over a range of activities. But in most cases developments such as this are not the principle objectives of any course of academic study.

Many students, however, are increasingly aware that the most significant thing for them about their higher education is securing some form of employment when it has finished. And here comes the tension. For those preparing for a profession, whether on a sandwich course or on a sequential pattern following the degree with a course of professional training, the matter is clear. They know within limits in what spheres of activity they are going to seek their career. But for very large numbers of students there is no necessary connection between what they have studied in higher education and what an employer requires of them. Each year about half of the details of appointments issued by the Central Services Unit of the University and Polytechnic Appointments Services do not specify the subject applicants should have studied, implying that a degree is higher general education. From that it is obvious that what their academic elders may expect of students may not tally with what the students see as being rewarding in the future.

Once more experiential learning can be of value. The inclusion of the educational potential of periods of work experience,
as an extension of the sandwich course idea, offers a way of
relating what is essentially a liberal education with career education. If a period of work and life experience was included in
each of the three years of the course, or in two, or even one if
other constraints were so limiting, students would be able to try
themselves out in different work contexts. This would also
encourage them to believe that their concern about employment
at the end of their course was shared by the institutions; the
organization of experiential learning on that scale, the direct
involvement of academic and counselling staff, the inevitable
commitment of resources for what would be a significant part of
the institution's responsibilities, would be immediately obvious
to students. It could bring higher education still closer.

In one College of Higher Education where this curriculum
approach has been developed there is evidence that it is highly
successful with students. It was studied with two others in a
DES-funded research project on Student Choice.[1] The first
indication is that the college concerned is almost embarrassed
by the number of applicants it receives each year – two or more
for each place available. Since a period of work experience is a
requirement of all degree courses, it is clearly no deterrent at the
lowest evaluation, and is indeed a possible attraction at the
other end of the scale. The second comes from students already
in the college, and concerns any doubts they might have enter-
tained about entering higher education at all. Of the students
who were not preparing for teaching (who are a special case for
this question), some 13 per cent, 66 per cent and 27 per cent
respectively for the three colleges surveyed, said they had
doubts about higher education because of the uncertainties
between the courses and possible careers. The report identified
'the same trend in each college . . . expressing some concern
over the link between the course and career . . .'

[1] C. Adelman and I. Gibbs, *A Study of Student Choice in the Context of Institutional Change*, Bulmersat College, Reading, 1979.

This further supports the case for the importance of experiential learning in revising the curriculum in an institution of higher education which wishes to attract additional categories of students while retaining the standards of attainment required for a first degree. Using experiential learning to provide career education in an academic course appeals to numbers of younger students, just as its inclusion as a basis for subsequent study has some appeal for older students. For younger students this needs strong emphasis. If part of the problem for higher education is to sustain its recruitment of 18 year olds when many of them are doubtful that further study can do anything much for them towards employment, then curriculum revision which increases the appeal of degree courses seems only common sense as institutional policy.

A period spent as an assistant to the curator of a country house open to the public can provide rich opportunities for studies in art and design, or history, or the management of tourism. Or, if the gardens and grounds were suitable, in ecology or the environment. A student who has work experience in the offices of a large company can develop a study of business and personnel management. Community work can offer opportunities for studying housing or town planning or sociology or economics or demography. In every case, in addition to documenting the work undertaken and subjecting it to critical analysis, the students can be required to give an account of the effect of the work on their perceptions of the assignment and on their understanding of themselves in relation to the demands being made upon them. Given proper academic guidance these kinds of experiences can lead to considerable new learning.

For older, experienced students the possibilities are even easier to envisage. The employee with considerable experience in a factory or engineering works can conduct systematic observations of an aspect of production or management as the basis for studies in psychology or sociology. The experienced secretary can make a study of internal information and communications systems. The voluntary worker with long experience of liaison with local authorities can study the workings of local government or of voluntary bodies. These few examples are merely indications of the wide ranging possibilities of extending the curriculum once the principle is accepted of assessing the learning which comes from experience.

After admission and curricula content, the next aspect to examine is mode of study. At several points earlier in this chapter proposals have rested on an assumption about modes of study which now needs to be explored: that people in employment or engaged in volunteer work cannot be full-time students.

There needs to be a break with the belief that, to be true to itself, higher education requires full-time students as its norm. By definition such a break is required if sufficient note is to be taken of the circumstances of potential students who are not drawn into the system at present. From the viewpoint of those students it means accepting a varying pattern of study so that domestic, employment and academic responsibilities can be fitted together as a satisfying, because satisfactory, whole. This is not to say that full-time study is any less important as the foundation for all the teaching and research of an academic institution. It is simply that the emphasis needs to change: part-time provision must become a major element. Here again experiential learning offers pointers. Either the independent study based on work experience, or the sandwich course concept using employment, voluntary work or hobbies or even domestic activity as a context for further learning, immediately introduces flexibility into a part-time programme, putting some of the timetabling in the hands of the students.

Flexible attendance requirements within part-time study are one step towards enabling students to control their own rhythm of study. Without them there is little or no possibility of convincing any potential student that institutions are taking them seriously. But arrangements need to be more varied still. Students need to be able to register for periods of full-time and/or part-time study within the same degree requirements, and to suspend their studies entirely for a period without any loss of time. There might well be detrimental effects on the student's work, as can happen to anyone who loses the momentum of study. But any such disadvantage would be for students to assess as they controlled the rhythm of their studies. It puts a great responsibility on them, an inevitable consequence of transferring the burden of decision from institution to individual; it is part of the price to be paid for part-time study.

Variations of this kind within the framework of a degree would mean, in effect, that a series of different tracks can be followed to the same end. A change of employment, home or marital status would not prevent the individual from complying with the degree regulations. So often, at present, cases appear of applicants who began their degree courses at 18-plus, withdrew for some reason or other, and then found that the studies they had satisfactorily completed would count for little or nothing if they enrolled for another course. Not surprisingly, all save the most determined can be discouraged. A course attendance pattern enabling different patterns of study could avoid just that kind of discouragement for some and, indeed, act as an incentive.

What existing regulations do not generally permit is the accumulation of results towards the eventual completion of a degree from courses completed under different modes of study spread out over varying lengths of time. From the student's point of view this would strengthen the same general development of making study easier to undertake and giving the student control of his own study. Cumulative study is a characteristic of modular full-time degree programmes such as those at Oxford Polytechnic or the City University, where a certain number of courses, or units, or modules, have to be completed each year. In a programme that enables students to take some of their courses in different disciplines each year, there has to be a cumulative system since, once the course has been completed in a discipline, it may not be studied again. Results are registered on the student's academic record. Part-time modular degrees use the same cumulative system. But, save in rare cases, and then usually through special dispensation, it is not possible to vary the number of courses which are taken in any one year, nor to take time off from study, returning to it later. What many students want is the kind of arrangement which is available through the Open University. There students know in advance how many course credits they require, and the number of course credits in different levels. Provided the courses are available, the students control their own work load and the length of time they will study by deciding which and how many courses to follow at any one time.

Cumulative rather than sequential study introduces the need for another facility: the transfer of academic results, or credits, from one institution to another. The Educational Credit Transfer Project referred to earlier published its final report in November 1979, and gives an account of present practices. It offers this definition of credit transfer: 'In the context of access to Higher and Further Education (HFE) credit transfer is a process whereby qualifications, part-qualifications and learning experiences are given recognition (or credit) to enable students to progress without having to repeat material or levels of study, to transfer from one course to another and to gain further educational experience and qualifications, thereby contributing to the maximisation of accumulated educational capital.'

There are three formal arrangements between institutions at national level. Agreements have been concluded between the Open University and the CNAA, and between the Open University and a number of other universities, which enable advanced standing (remission of course, and shortening the length of study required) to be accorded in appropriate cases to students wishing to transfer between those institutions. The Open University also has schemes with the Technician Education Council and the Business Education Council which enable students to accumulate credits and transfer. Apart from the occasional case, none of this applies to part-time study for degrees in universities. By and large, and apart from London University's Birkbeck College, part-time degree study is not available in universities, apart from the Open University. So although the principle of credit transfer is established within the HFE system it does not apply generally to part-time study.

The Educational Credit Transfer study shows that most of the credit transfer which occurs at present between institutions of higher education is largely to do with admission of advanced standing, entering directly in to the second or perhaps third year of a course on the basis of previous study, and is primarily concerned with Open University course credits as the currency of transfer. There is no evidence of transfer between other institutions save on an individual and occasional basis; there is no recognized system.

There is an obvious difficulty. As the Final Report put it, 'However, a major concern in admitting students with advanced standing remains, that of ensuring a realistic and appropriate match between previous courses and those for which admission is being sought so that students are not disadvantaged.' Thus a head of department who is considering accepting as a student someone who has already completed two years of degree-level study in his subject, but who had not followed the course studied by the third-year students he would be joining, faces a problem; if the former study is not an appropriate match with his own courses and he accepts the applicant, he will either be saying that it does not matter that the applicant has not completed the first two years of the course, or requiring special arrangements for his tuition in those areas where the applicant is deficient.

From the individual student's viewpoint however, it does not matter that credit transfer presents considerable difficulties to institutions; its availability would make a world of difference to his view of what higher education can offer. At present its absence is an undoubted deterrent to some potential applicants. And this is not just a matter of individual preference. These days a considerable number of potential students are liable to be moved from one post to another in different parts of the country within the same company or organization, or may find they need to move home to secure promotion. It is a condition of life for many. It is highly unsatisfactory that people who are affected by this social and career mobility should find that part of the price they have to pay is that the courses of higher education which they have completed already are not acceptable at the same valuation in another institution. Literally, they have wasted their time. This is nothing whatsoever to do with what they have learnt and their level of attainment. It is all to do with the regulations under which degrees are taught, which in turn is a consequence of the way the courses have been designed. For the hypothetical part-time student, that is precisely the point. So credit transfer is a facility which stands as a symbol of the part-time students: so long as it remains as difficult as at present to transfer from one institution to another without loss of study time, then the conclusion must be that the part-time student has not been accepted as a major responsibility of higher education. For just as long, many of those potential part-time students will not trouble to turn to higher education because it seems to ignore the realities of their lives.

Once again experiential learning has something to offer. Procedures for judging the learning derived from life and work experience could be used to assess the level of knowledge and skills derived from taught courses. This could overcome the problem, cited from the Credit Transfer Study, of 'ensuring a realistic match between previous courses and those for which admission is being sought, so that students may not be disadvantaged.' Admission tutors could discover whether there was an acceptable match for themselves; they would not be attempting to find a match between different syllabuses. They would not be taking anything on trust, but making their own judgements. And since the nature of institutions in Britain and their courses is such that it is almost inconceivable that credit transfer on a course basis could ever be established across the higher education system, this particular use which could be made of assessment procedures evolved for experiential learning could be of considerable significance.

Short courses are now playing an increasingly important part in the academic work of universities and polytechnics. Much of the impetus for this development has come from the need of industry and commerce to give many of their personnel systematically planned periods of re-training. Larger numbers of people from every sphere of employment are liable to become involved in these forms of mid-life education. The level of work involved in re-training courses is bound to vary greatly: some will be at very advanced levels of postgraduate work; others at about undergraduate level; and then still others will be at sub-degree level. From every point of view it is clear that wherever possible links must be made between this form of educational provision, and first-degree studies. Not to do so ignores the common interests of industry, commerce and higher education. It might be possible for some re-training courses to be accepted as evidence for matriculation. Others might be seen as preparatory courses for a degree programme, a bridge between the present attainment levels of employees on short courses and those required for further study. It could even be that within a part-time degree structure which included the facilities for assessing experiential learning, some of the work completed in short courses could be used as the basis for further study in an Independent Study, as suggested previously. Organic links would then be forged between two essential educational parties – employer and academic – in the interests of employees.

There would seem no reason why sub-degree courses should not be designed outside the re-training requirements of employers, but with the same opportunities subsequently relating one level of study to another for adults who wished to use a stepping-stone approach to their studies. And if the cumulative principle could be applied to those lowest levels, another incentive for further study would be given to groups of men and women who are inclined to think that higher education studies are right outside their grasp and remote from them. Staying as far apart as they are today deprives both potential students and institutions of what each needs: study for students, students for institutions. Bringing them together means developing as many varieties of part-time study as the circumstances of students require. That cannot be done without a major institutional commitment to part-time courses, bringing the part-time student into the mainstream of academic work. It means a fundamental shift in academic responsibility. Some of the institutional implications of this are explored in the next chapter.

The gap between part-time students and mainstream higher education is indicated by the present financial arrangements which demonstrate how sections of the population are given little encouragement to study further. Mandatory grants for full-time students are the mainstream flow; discretionary grants for part-time students are a relatively small flow from a minor tributary. At the present time of financial constraints that minor tributary is in danger of drying up altogether, as local authorities trim their budgets. This disparity between the financial support available for full-time mainly younger students and part-time adult learners symbolizes the difference in status accorded to the two groups, and is a measure of yet another shift which is necessary before the gap can be reduced between higher education which institutions offer and the numbers and kinds of people who use it.

Within the present structure of student grants there appears to be no acceptable principle on which to base the differential treatment of part- and full-time students. It has grown up pragmatically and remains, despite continual pressure to change it. There may be strong arguments for saying that in total the present amount of financial support for all students ranks high amongst all the calls there are on public expenditure. As an economic reality there is little likelihood of that amount being increased, even if it was desirable to do so. If that is a reasonable premise for discussing students grants, it follows that equitable redistribution of grant aid needs to be considered for all students, be they part-time or full-time. One simple approach would be to award an entitlement for financial support for a given period of full-time study or its part-time equivalent to each man and woman at the point when they began a higher education course. Beyond that period a system of student loans could be available for those who wished to use them rather than paying fees directly, either themselves or through some sponsoring academic institution or employer.

The effect of such a development on full-time study can only be guessed. If the number of full-time students drops as is anticipated, and the present levels of student grants are maintained, even allowing for inflation, it might be possible to extend comparable support to part-time students without altering the present entitlement of full-time students for the duration of their course (usually three, but sometimes four, years). However, if the number of full-time students does not fall as sharply as is generally assumed, to permit such a painless redeployment of resources it might be necessary to investigate the implications of reducing the entitlement of full-time students to make room for an equivalent entitlement for part-time students. Indeed something of the kind would seem inevitable if the principle of financial support is to be applied to all the population. Sub-degree work leading into degree studies illustrates the point. Revisions of financial policy of this kind are a very large undertaking. The political as well as economic and national housekeeping implications are great. But again, if the point is taken seriously that the future of higher education lies in doing more of what it does not do much of at present, and less of what it presently does, then changes in financial as well as institutional and academic policy have to be made.

The institutional focus for these questions comes in the next chapter. But for individuals, access, course content, study opportunities, the use made of existing knowledge, and financial support, have to be set in the wider context. It is no good going to the trouble of providing new courses and opportunities if applicants cannot find out about them easily. Clearly a national information service is going to be essential. For example, on the question of student choice, the evidence given from Student Choice project, cited earlier, establishes that, in the three colleges studied, the college prospectus was the most important source of information for the great majority of students when applying for places. This is corroborated by the study of factors influencing entry to a university, polytechnic or college of education which was referred to in Chapter 2. It agrees with what most families would say whose relations have gone to study in higher education. But finding out what is available is a major problem. Most students in higher education have been helped in the early stages of considering possibilities at schools and further education colleges in being referred to prospectuses. It is the stock-in-trade for careers staff and sixth-form tutors and advisers. But the volume of information now available about different institutions, and about different courses within institutions, is almost overwhelming. To interpret that information comprehensively for each individual making an enquiry is literally beyond the competence of any careers officer. This is true for those who need little or no persuading from their schools and colleges about applying for places. The problems in introducing the possibilities to those who do not readily consider them are subtle and acute.

Despite the mountains of information available, if institutions are really serious about recruiting from additional constituencies they face the same problems as any advertiser: of convincing the consumer that what the advertiser is purveying is what suits the individual. The first requirement is to try to arouse interest.

The Educational Credit Transfer Project commissioned a paper on Adult and Continuing Education which looked at existing information services and commented on what a national information service should take as its brief. More or less simultaneously, the Advisory Council for Adult and Continuing Education published *Links to Learning*, a report on educational information, and advisory and counselling services for adults. It, too, surveyed existing services and made recommendations for the future. Although Educational Credit Transfer was primarily interested in an information service about educational transfer, necessarily such a service would be incorporated in an overall information service and so its findings are pertinent to the argument of this Chapter. The same is true of ACACE's report. It was concerned with the information for adults about every aspect of educational possibilities and so includes higher education.

Both these reports make clear the present very extensive range of information services. *Links to Learning* lists eight avenues for the dissemination of educational information at national level:

- The British Library research project on the potential for a national information bank for community information organisation
- The government financed 'Credit Transfer Feasibility Study' of the potential for a national information bank on accredited courses with data on alternative entry qualifications
- The Open University's student enquiry service which frequently extends beyond the University's own courses
- The 'Joblibraries' of the Manpower Services Commission
- The national telephone referral service offered by the Adult Literacy Support Services Fund
- The information service of the National Institute of Adult Education
- The Higher Education Advisory Centre
- The Further Education Information Service

There are collaborative projects in many parts of the UK where local authorities and institutions organize special information services using mobile caravans, run stalls and drop-in centres in shopping precincts, publish pamphlets, take part in phone-in programmes on local radio stations; the variety is endless. There are the Local Authorities' Careers Guidance Services. The Manpower Services Commission offers advice and counselling through its various centres. Educational Guidance Services for adults can be found in some parts of the country. The difficulty is that the provision varies greatly from one part of the country to another. Few of the schemes offer the comprehensive service required. Generally the funding is not secure, and the performance is bound to be somewhat erratic. There is no nationally co-ordinated scheme to provide the same level of service.

Any future proposal needs to confront the problem as presented succinctly in the paper commissioned for the Educational Credit Transfer Project: 'The crux of the problem is this: how does information about a range of particular educational and training opportunities reach adults, learners and potential learners?' This raises two sets of questions: on information accessing and on information providing. Neither is easy to answer, for answers must suit the circumstances of the potential students, just as courses and teaching and timetabling need to be arranged to fit them. Often these men and women are looking for a way of changing their lives, but they may have little confidence about their own abilities, may often be unaware of their own needs and may have great difficulty in trying to find things out for themselves. They tend to want concrete information which they can then begin to interpret according to their own circumstances. They are likely to be ambivalent about the education they have already received and yet may have quite traditional ideas about what is involved if they decide to enrol. Naturally for many the prime interest is likely to be connected with job and career prospects. Increasingly for a number of women that can mean finding ways of making either a first or a second start on a career. But equally the search for personal satisfaction through additional study which is the motivation of many potential students can mean an uncertainty about how to present their interests. Above all, perhaps, they are highly resistant to attempts at persuasion.

From the potential student's point of view, then, an impersonal information service and a personal, optional guidance service meet the twin needs of information accessing and information providing. Ideally an information service about higher education should be as familiar a service as the news and weather reports. It should be used as confidently and easily as finding out about entertainments or prices in the shops. Anyone ought to be able to pick up a telephone, or use a television linked system like Ceefax, to make the first set of inquiries about courses, their eligibility, the location and so on, and then be able to visit an educational guidance and information centre if necessary, and so pass on to an institution. There would appear to be no difficulty in principle in establishing such a computerized system. It is happening for other services; it should begin to happen for education. Perhaps that can stand as a symbol for the kinds of development which are necessary before there can be much chance of additional groups of potential students becoming actual students. A computerized information and guidance system would reiterate the message that education was part of the world they inhabit, and not something which was irrelevant to it.

Different ways of gaining access to higher education, different ways of studying, different ways of defining areas of study, different ways of finding out about courses, they all amount to a significant extension of the present provision of higher education. And they are all necessary, if institutions are going to recruit sufficient students to keep their work alive, and if students are to receive sufficient service for the money they pay in taxes to support them. It is extremely unlikely that they can simply be added to what is already provided. The introduction of these policies is likely to depend on an institution's willingness to give up something else first. There is no more severe test.

6

Introducing the Programmes

The developments outlined in the previous chapter offer opportunities to more people for benefiting from studying for degrees. They also offer institutions additional opportunities for sustaining their recruitment. Each development concerns either academic organization or the curriculum itself. Part-time study is the basic organizational issue; the basic curriculum issue is the recognition of knowledge and skills whatever their source. Credit accumulation – the facility for completing courses over a period of time, having the results recorded and stored until the requisite number of courses has been completed – clearly depends on administrative and academic decisions. So does credit transfer, enabling students to complete studies by taking courses in more than one institution without loss of time through needing to repeat courses. All pose far-reaching policy questions.

The argument throughout this book is that they have to be faced, and this means institutions being prepared to re-examine their work which in many cases is likely to require systematically devising programmes for staff development and retraining. It is difficult to see how a better match can otherwise be achieved between individuals and institutions.

The case for the search for a better match can be put by quoting from the final report in 1976 of Unesco's Committee of

Experts on Post Secondary Education for Persons Gainfully Employed: 'The timing of post secondary education during a person's career should be a function of his occupational objectives, his interests, needs and personal abilities in the area of general, social and civic education, and should not be limited to any specific time frame. There are, however, critical times for education associated with retraining through a person's lifetime.' That is tacitly proposing an extension of present higher education provision, pointing to new kinds of service. Part-time study, periodic study, study which can accelerate different interests for people of different ages and stages in their personal and professional occupational development, these are all implied.

That extension is set in its context by the OECD paper, 'Education and Working Life' (1977):

The very strong individual demand for higher education, which is now spreading among adults, continues in large measure to be governed by the social and economic status that it has acquired. The sum total of these demands is still rising. Although its composition changes in relation to students' perceptions of career prospects in different occupations, the total demand for higher education appears to be autonomous and not conditioned by specific prospects. It shows little sign of being contained by or adapting itself to the currently and prospectively limited and uncertain overall employment prospects for graduates, especially in the public sector, including teaching, which until recently has absorbed a very high proportion of them. A central problem is to what extent and by what means this demand can be satisfied: on one hand it is recognized that higher education has a vital contribution to make to economic development and employment and that its cultural objectives are specially important: yet on the other hand it has to be borne in mind that there are limitations on resources, that other levels of education have competing claims, and that many countries are concerned to provide a more equitable access to education within society.

The Robbins Report is an earlier presentation of similar sentiments:

> In our submission there are at least four objectives essential to any properly balanced system [of higher education]. We begin with instruction in skills suitable to play a part in the general division of labour. We put this first, not because we regard it as the most important, but because we think that it is sometimes ignored or undervalued . . . (p. 25).
>
> But secondly, while emphasising that here is no betrayal of values when institutions of higher education teach what will be of some practical use, we must postulate that what is taught should be taught in such a way as to promote the general powers of the mind . . . (p. 26).
>
> Thirdly, we must name the advancement of learning. There are controversial issues here concerning the balance between teaching and researching in the various institutions of higher education and the distribution of research between these institutions and other bodies . . . But the search for truth is an essential function of institutions of higher education and the role of education is itself most vital when it partakes of the nature of discovery . . . (p. 27).
>
> Finally, there is a function that is more difficult to describe concisely, but that is none the less fundamental; the transmission of a common culture and common standards of citizenship (p. 28).

In different ways these various extracts are urging higher education to play its unique part in the overall movement towards what has come to be known as continuing education though that is not what Robbins had in mind. To do so in Britain means adding to existing facilities for study. What is needed is a higher education system which works like a motorway. The ultimate destination is clear (a degree), known and can be reached assuming there are no mechanical breakdowns. But it is not necessary to begin the journey where the motorway begins (admission with advanced standing); it can be joined at well-marked points along the route. Nor is it necessary to proceed the full length of the journey without a pause (periodic study). There are resting places along the way. And there are also exits from which it is possible to meander for a while, along by-roads, or to take time out from the main journey and do something else other than travelling – picnicking, shopping, sightseeing, or just sleeping (accumulation of credits). At the chosen time, the motorway can be joined again either at the same place, or further along if the meanderings have followed more or less the same direction (credit for additional knowledge acquired). The time taken over the journey is in the control of the traveller (full-time or part-time study). It is even possible to cross to another motorway which may go to the same destination (transfer credit). Provided the traveller observes the highway code (degree regulations), then how and when he reaches his destination is his decision. Not all destinations can be reached by travelling along motorways (some institutions would not be making these arrangements for study) and so it is up to the traveller to decide what kind of journey he wants to make. Motorway travel may be very convenient for him except that it does not take him where he wants to go. In which case he has to settle for a less convenient route in order to get where he wants (select either convenient mode of study or, if necessary, the institution which offers the course required) and settle down to the journey. At present only a very small number of higher education institutions are served by this kind of motorway system. Most are at the end of access roads which have no entries or exits along them. For the future we need sufficient universities, polytechnics and colleges to be marked on the motorway map so that as nearly as possible everyone, wherever they live, can use the motorway system to reach one of them.

This could be interpreted as an arid, instrumental view of higher education; setting the award of a degree as the 'destination' and ignoring the pursuit of truth, or the delights of studying in favourite subjects. But passengers along the motorway can use their journey for whatever purpose they choose. The vital thing for them is that they can make their journey for their own convenience. It needs to be the same in higher education. Between them, the range of institutions needs to be able to provide for the convenience of all different categories of students.

What does that mean in practice? Clearly, there have to be substantial adaptations and changes to present arrangements. For example, an institution could offer the full range of opportunities. Applicants without matriculation qualifications could propose themselves as degree students and be accepted or rejected on the basis of assessments of their knowledge and skills. Some could then join the regularly provided classes and lectures as either full-time or part-time students. Some might attempt to devise a course of study which fitted their particular needs and interests in consultation with tutors as a part of their degree programmes, because they could not find what they wanted from the courses provided. For some it could be that towards the end of their course independent study occupied all their study time. Other applicants might have studied elsewhere, and would ask for that work to be assessed and accepted on a credit transfer basis towards the award of a degree. In other words in view of previous study they would be seeking a shortened course. Some full-time students could be seeking periods of work experience which would provide them with opportunities for learning which would count towards the degree. Part-time students might be seeking assessment of their learning from their daily employment, and under tutorial guidance using it as a basis for further study at work. Both part-time and full-time students could suspend their studies for a while, picking up where they left off. Some part-time students might wish to become full-time students for a period, and then revert to part-time study. Full-time students might wish to study part-time for a while. Another institution could offer facilities for the assessment of experiential learning for entry to their full-time courses, allowing part-time students to fit in if they could, but making no further adaptations to their practice. Yet another could offer special programmes for part-time students, providing preparatory courses with opportunities for backdating the commencement of degree studies if the work completed on the preparatory course merited it. Universities, colleges and polytechnics could all introduce these extensions to present provision if they wished – a sufficient number will need to if higher education is to stay intact and come to terms with the needs of the people it exists to serve.

Coming to terms, however, requires changes: in attitudes to potential students, and in the use of available resources. Changes in attitudes means accepting that different additional constituencies of students have different requirements from the traditional 18 plus entrants. All the ways institutions can extend their provisions just mentioned depends upon that acceptance. It also requires a changed perspective of what constitutes academic learning. The recognition of knowledge and skills acquired from life and work experience involves accepting that unorganized, unplanned, incidental learning can lead to academic attainment levels which are in some cases a proper basis for degree study and in others equivalent to parts of a degree course. This brings a substantial alteration in the professional roles of academic staff. The institutional changes presupposed by new provisions for different categories of students require a redeployment of resources. The administration services necessary to deal with the work arising from the introduction of additional opportunities for study are considerable; in, for example, admission and registration, and record keeping. This switch in financial resources can be relatively painless, if student numbers can be sustained by attracting new kinds of students to compensate for the absolute decline in the numbers of 18 plus applicants which is bound to come for many institutions. However difficult they may be, changes then amount to doing less of what is done at present, but filling the space with new developments. It will be far harder if student numbers drop, whatever may be done to attract new clienteles.

But that sharpens the significance of trying to attract them, and puts a greater premium on institutional and academic changes.

An institution can only make significant changes with the support of its staff. Hence the need for some specific preparation. Unfortunately there could hardly be a worse time than the present for facing staff with the need to change their ways. As numbers of traditional 18-plus students decline from 1985 onwards, numbers of staff must also decline unless additional students are forthcoming from other sections of the population. The signs are already there to be read. In polytechnics and colleges, problems of holding numbers of students in balance with numbers of staff at the ratio of roughly ten to one has brought a considerable number of redundancies, and voluntary or compulsory retirement. Universities are now being forced to find solutions to the same issues: reduced funding and so reduced unemployment.

Reactions to these developments vary as widely as the people who face them. Academics may be very able in their own fields, but when confronted with personal problems they are not necessarily any better at dealing with them than anyone else. Many would say that because they lead such protected lives they are often less able to deal with such difficulties than others. Steel workers, miners and public authority employees and their trade unions, for example, can react aggressively to policies which threaten their jobs. Even when the threat is not dismissal but a requirement to change from one job to another, the resistance can be just as fierce. Academics are expected to react differently to similar circumstances because of their intellectual ability but that does not mean they do. Like everyone else, they find some kinds of change threatening, for it introduces uncertainty. There are two sources of uncertainty, each creating insecurity: the question of continued employment, and the nature of employment itself. Obviously the two are linked. There is the direct threat to employment as student numbers decline. To sustain recruitment may mean significant alterations to duties undertaken, threatening the nature of employment. For most people both kinds of threat are difficult to live with.

There are currently several ways of reducing staff: temporary appointments can be terminated, provided the terms of employment permit it in the Employment Protection Act; redundancy inducements can increase the number of retirements; posts can be frozen; short-term appointments cover serious gaps. One way and another, institutions can contrive to bring numbers down, but this inevitably creates internal tensions. This underscores the problems of a static staff going stale because of lack of promotion chances and losing drive and experiencing mounting frustration.

This raises the question of tenure as a condition of appointment. In Britain the majority of academic staff hold their appointments with what is in effect a lifetime entitlement, in sharp contrast to the practices of other countries. Whatever may be the arguments in favour of it as safeguarding essential academic freedoms, it is now highly controversial. If absolute numbers of students decline, requiring reductions in staff numbers, institutions will simply have to manage as best they can with those already holding appointments on the assumption that retirements and resignations will suffice. An increase in short-term appointments without tenure would seem essential. Although it has been assumed that existing permanent posts would be unaffected, present investigations into the exact legal implications of tenure are now arousing anxiety among the professional associations, the Association of University Teachers and the National Association of Teachers in Further and Higher Education.

Simultaneously, the internal log-jam produces other anxieties. Waiting for another's retirement for the gratifications of promotion is a frustrating business. For most such frustration is not conducive to effective teaching or academic work. The dangers are obvious: present dissatisfaction tends to make it difficult to contemplate the possible satisfactions from developments which otherwise would not be at all welcome, even though those developments may be the way to avert threats to employment.

The nature of employment then becomes a key issue for established academics. Demands are bound to be made on members of a relatively static staff to undertake different work even without any of the kinds of institutional developments sketched earlier. Some staff are bound to find themselves asked to accept unfamiliar teaching assignments which they may not relish, and relieved of doing those they cherish most. They could easily have to teach courses in which they do not feel thoroughly competent according to their own beliefs about academic standards, despite considerable preparation. Some of these feelings can be muted if changes in teaching duties are accompanied by new responsibilities in another sphere, but within a static staff that is unlikely. Instead of the stimulus from anticipated promotion, there can be the deadening weight of disappointment and resigned acceptance of being in a rut.

However, the changes described in this chapter can be viewed as a way of expanding opportunities for academics to develop their work. So, seen in a different light, these very uncertainties can be stimulating. Changes can be presented in positive terms, provided that the necessity for them is recognized and accepted, even though not welcomed. If the need for them can be accepted, then the consequent extension of higher education provision, which is the general theme running through this book, could offer great opportunities for academics.

Staff preparation becomes the central matter. This is another way of saying that higher education needs to strike out and find a future developing substantial areas which are relatively untried and unfamiliar, which therefore creates very demanding work. That poses squarely the question of re-training. There is a wry coincidence here; many of the potential students who may boost the future recruitments of institutions will be seeking some form of re-training, and many of the academic staff who will be expected to teach them will be themselves in similar need of re-training to undertake their new roles. For the most part, training for those new teaching requirements cannot be met by leaving things to chance. That tends to happen in education all to often, it has to be said, and is almost certainly responsible for the low regard many have for education. For all its talk of professionalism, it seems too often to be so unprofessional. A staff re-training programme too is required to bridge the gap between what higher education is doing at present and what it needs to attempt for the future.

However, not everyone can undertake everything. Any re-training programme is bound to be an opportunity for some individuals to redefine their roles. Earlier it was argued that institutions could improve their teaching substantially if they took into account the various stages of development of their students and the effect of the relationship between different aspects of that development on their readiness for learning. The same applies to academic staff. An individual who finds it difficult to conceive of his teaching task as serving as a resource to be consulted and used at the behest of students may feel quite secure when declaiming in lectures authoritatively. He could find working with experienced adult students not merely anti-pathetic but threatening. This would not be a matter for criti-cism, but a reflection of the teacher's own characteristics at his particular stage of development. He might well teach more effectively if he paid as much attention to his own teaching methods as he paid to the work produced by his students. Encouragement to do so could well be the most important result from any programme of further professional training that he undertook. But it could easily be said that he would never teach the experienced student adults confidently. Staff preparation means recognizing that.

The point is obvious in any considered scheme of re-training, and yet is rarely considered as a matter of professional responsi-bility. It is now important to do so, because it bears directly on any attempt to alter an institution's provision. Many ex-perienced men and women will only be prepared to consider undertaking unfamiliar work which does not feel entirely appropriate if there is time for cautious discussion and thorough exploration. Even then it is quite unrealistic to expect at the beginning that more than a relatively small number will respond positively to being asked to do something different. Switching from one professional role to another within the same field can seem like being asked to become someone else. For some it is asking the impossible; for others it is possible; for others still it is a stimulus to be welcomed with gratitude. The range of responses simply illustrates the need to take seriously the different stages of the staff's development. It also shows the scope of a programme of professional development in an academic institution which sets out to develop its provision. For example, where the developing part-time study becomes a major concern, staff will need to review their courses and redesign some of them, moving beyond questions of academic organization to the curriculum itself. Where an institution begins to develop academic programmes which involve any aspect of experiential learning, staff are bound to find themselve engaged in a fundamental reconsideration of their roles. Some will find that harder and more trying than others. This is why some systematic preparation is a necessary pre-condition for extending the present provision. In the process of determining how to undertake extensions, inevitably every other aspect of an institution's provision will be reviewed. An institution would be trying to redefine its purpose, inevitably to the alarm of some older members.

The place to begin considering the effects for staff of new developments is with access to courses, with admission procedures and regulations. In principle the academic staff's concern is straightforward: a matter of attainment at the time of application and of prophecy about subsequent attainment. The yardstick currently employed for both in Britain is the 'A' Level. On the whole the arrangement works fairly well because everyone concerned knows how the 'A' Level examination works. In practice admission tutors are often prepared to back their own judgement whatever the evidence produced from 'A' Levels. Any insider can produce stories about candidates who were offered places conditional upon achieving a certain point score in 'A' Level examinations and who, having failed to achieve them, are then awarded a place notwithstanding. Sometimes this is because at interview the admission tutor was sufficiently impressed with the candidate to decide there and then that he was worth a place even though the official offer was conditional. Sometimes it is because there are vacancies to be filled. Sometimes it can be because the candidate's school or college considers results to be out of line with reasonable expectations, writes to this effect to the college or university concerned and successfully reverses the rejection.

That is a vital point to establish in exploring different access rates to higher education. For if academic staff are willing to rely on their judgements in some circumstances when deciding on admissions, there would appear to be no reason why they should not rely on it in others: when considering the learning derived from life and work experience. To do so means accepting the validity of learning whatever its source. Individuals should thus be recognized as to what they know and can do regardless of how they have arrived at those attainments. Although this must mean academics accepting that learning can take place without reference to formal educational institutions, it in no way weakens their position as assessors of learning. The responsibility for academic standards in higher education remains with them. This is all the more important as society's demands increase for judgements about competencies and levels of academic attainment. And while professional bodies and large corporations are increasingly seeing themselves as competent authorities to make these judgments, ultimately it is the academic institutions which carry this public responsibility.

Admission procedures are simply part of this more general responsibility for assessment and judgement which needs to be developed systematically. The first step in the assessment of uncertificated knowledge must be to identify the learning acquired which is claimed to be of either matriculation standard or degree level. Then that learning, the knowledge and skills identified, can be related to the degree programme the applicant wishes to follow so that the connections between the two can be clearly articulated. Evidence for the acquisition of the learning must be documented as a means of establishing its validity. The learning can then be measured, to determine its quantity and quality. It can then be evaluated, weighed academically as equating with matriculation requirements, or with some of the requirements for parts of the degree. The final stage is to compile an accurate record of the results of the assessment in a form which enables an independent inquirer to use it as a record (see Chapter 4, figure 5). Following these steps enables an applicant to produce what was described in Chapter 4 on the American approaches to some of these matters as Portfolio Assessment. In effect, it means writing an educational autobiography, fully documented, presented so as to show what has been learned and its source. Ideally the preparation of a portfolio is undertaken in a class with the guidance of a tutor. The benefits of this are abundantly clear from the experience in America of both students and tutors, and are corroborated by my own direct observation of them. Frequently it happens that during discussions and attempts to produce a coherent and systematic account of what he knows, a student's powers of analysis and reflection develop, enabling him to articulate far more than he ever realized that he knew. However it is completed, a portfolio provides staff with evidence on which to make judgements. Whether assessments are being made for admission or for learning derived from work experience during the course, this autobiographical approach is equally appropriate as a significant element.

There are and there have always been admission procedures for taking account of other qualifications which are considered comparable to 'A' Levels. Any admission documents will provide lists of equivalent qualifications; and they tend to be very long indeed. Further, there are ways of considering applications from candidates without any formal examinations to their credit. (Chapter 5 showed some of the precedents for developing admission procedures.) Each university has its own conventions and the CNAA provides guidance for institutions. The present institutional position over admissions to degree courses is therefore clear. If an institution teaching a CNAA degree wishes to admit students lacking the normal entry qualifications, there is no apparent reason why it should not develop an alternative system whereby it would make academic assessments of the knowledge and skills claimed by unqualified applicants. Universities establish their own rules for admission. Each one could, if it were so minded, set up similar arrangements for the assessment of applicants without formal qualifications.

A policy of accepting assessments of uncertified learning for admission qualifications has to be based on valid and reliable assessment procedures. The staff with the responsibility for assessing uncertified learning have their own academic experience and professional judgement to rely on – and precedent but nothing else. There are no syllabuses to help them plot the candidate's knowledge. They can obtain references from others to verify the accuracy of statements made by the candidate, but they do need some means of establishing what reliance they can place on any judgements of referees about the quality of the candidate's knowledge. They can set written tests and conduct orals, both under supervision: they can set essays to be written at home. There is nothing they may not attempt in collecting the evidence they require in order to come to a decision about whether the candidate has the same capacity to study as those who matriculated through the conventional route. But they need to decide how to set about it, effectively, reliably, to the satisfaction of both the candidate and their academic colleagues. The candidate is claiming competence in certain areas of knowledge. The academic task is to approve or disprove that claim.

Many admission tutors could well claim that this is more or less what they do now when they back their own judgements rather than examination results. Usually that means relying on impressions gained from an interview and from various confidential references – and in most cases there is an extensive educational record to support them. However, investigating claims to uncertified knowledge as a method of admission for older men and women is very different. What educational records there are likely to be out of date, giving only a general impression of the abilities quite unrelated to the stage of development of the candidate at the time of application. Current formal educational references are by definition not available. An interview, even when most thoroughly conducted, is unlikely to prove adequate for making an overall judgement.

This makes clear the need for a system as an integral part of the institution's policy, to ensure consistency when, in the nature of things, candidates are going to show marked inconsistencies one with another. Different institutions may evolve different systems, and the balance between what the candidate is required to produce as evidence, and what the institution requires in the form of entrance examinations will vary. The full procedure can only be devised after careful planning, experiment and continual checking of results against other procedures. In effect this is a major exercise in staff training; in the process other considerations are likely to emerge. The staff concerned are bound to find themselves considering the courses they teach as a reference point for the assessments. If they are to accept students lacking the conventional preparation, they are likely to need to clarify what they expect of students not only at the beginning of courses, but also when they end. The aims and purposes of courses will be scrutinized as well as the syllabuses. As they do so, some will find that although the syllabus seems precise, it is not clear what the students are expected to be able to do as a result of the course. This will put them in a better position to tackle the other issues arising from the acceptance of experiential learning: the connections between admission and subsequent study, the place of assessment of experiential learning derived from practical experience within degrees, and admission with advanced standing or remission of course.

In one sense this third issue, admission with advanced standing, is perhaps the easiest to deal with. A decision has to be made as to whether a student has mastered the work of a course without being taught for it. That can be settled by an end-of-course examination – the challenge exam idea. That cannot work, however, where what a candidate claims to know does not fall neatly within the syllabus of an existing course. In those cases it could well be that the procedure already described for considering for admission candidates without formal qualifications could prove appropriate. But, again, there would need to be a recognized system as institution policy if academic staff are to have confidence in the procedures as part of the study programme. Once students have been enrolled for a degree, the institution is responsible for assessing their learning whatever its course. Confidence in procedures is essential if confidence in standards is to be preserved.

One of the issues arising from admitting students without formal qualifications is the connection between what they know at entry and the course which they wish to study. Broadly, one of two approaches can be used. One is to conceive of the assessment of experiential learning as a means of relating what applicants know to the particular courses they wish to follow. For example, if a lawyer's clerk wanted to read for a law degree or perhaps a degree in business administration, the assessment of what he claimed to know could be based on a fairly precise comparison with the content of some of the courses he intended to follow. Or if it were someone wishing to read for a history or English degree, the same procedure could be adopted. However, an application for history or English could also be considered differently. It might be that the periods of history (or literature) studied in the institution were relatively unfamiliar to an applicant who was claiming to be well versed in other periods or sources. In this case no direct comparison could be made between the content of courses to be studied and what the applicant knew. Instead a judgement would need to be made about the applicant's general grasp of the conceptual structure of the study and so his capacity to study in new areas of the discipline.

This second approach is also needed when an applicant is wishing to study in areas which may not be directly related to what he knows already. Here some judgement has to be made about the general level of academic competence in both knowledge and study skills on the basis of what an applicant already knows. Whatever the approach adopted, the process needs to provide a reliable way of making academically valid judgements about present levels of attainment and of capacity for further study.

There is a further consideration which arises from the use of experiential learning for admission purposes – its connection with independent study as a component in a degree. (The size of the component depends on a consideration of the depth and breadth of the study proposed. It could be a small option, a major option, or even a full degree.) In the previous chapter, the point was made that in some cases applicants whose successful claim to knowledge and skills gains them entry to a degree may well have fairly clear ideas of what they wish to study but find it is not provided for in any course on offer. By working with a member of the academic staff familiar with the proposed study area, a student can devise a programme which compares favourably with the taught courses in related areas and proves acceptable academically as a degree component. Here again, there needs to be a clearly laid down procedure for institutions to ensure the maintenance of academic standards whatever the mode of learning and give a necessary sense of security to students and staff alike. This is an instance of using uncertified knowledge as a basis for further study.

There are many ways that 'uncertified' knowledge can be used as a basis for further study and Independent Study can be a helpful compendium description of them all. Some part-time students might well wish to use their daily place of work as the context for further study, through investigating, say, the social dynamics of the people they work with and relating this to particular theories, or making development work in the use of materials as a basis for critical study, or making a case study of human problems encountered during work in community service. Each of those who could be directed by a tutor to ensure that the work met the required academic critieria. Others might wish to take their employment as the point of departure and pursue an aspect as a pure academic study which did not fit into any existing course. A bank clerk might be interested in studying the development of banking in a third-world country, but find that no existing course coincided with that interest. Under tutorial guidance, such a study could be quite possible. The institution would maintain its full academic control over the material being studied. It would be undertaken only with the agreement of a tutor, who retained responsibility for supervising the work and for its assessment. All the normal academic requirements would be met, except that the work did not originate from a formally taught course. The experience at Lancaster University, where this facility is already available, shows that it has some considerable appeal for full-time undergraduates; there have also been interesting developments at the North East London Polytechnic[1] where this facility is available shows that it has already some appeal for full-time undergraduates. There is every reason to think that it would be a considerable attraction to the newer kinds of students which this book is pursuing.

In addition to independent study, there are a number of other possible ways of integrating experiential learning with academic study in institutions. Any extension of the sandwich course method of interleaving periods of practical experience with periods of formal study can introduce similar opportunities. To do so, however, requires a definition of the purpose of the practical experience in general and a fairly

---

[1] Keith Percy and Paul Ramsden, *Independent Study: Two Example from Higher Education*, Guildford: Society for Research into Higher Education, 1980.

precise prescription of the learning tasks the student is required to accomplish. The practical experience itself has to become a source of learning, like any other course, the results of which are assessed like any other. This has to be the case whatever the activity the institution is authorizing, whether in industry or commerce, the professions, or voluntary work, or home-based. It is equally applicable to full-time and part-time study. Procedurally this requires a similar systematic approach to the assessments for admission (see Chapter 4). All the six steps in the sequence for that assessment system need to be completed, but the order may need varying. Every institution will need to make differing arrangements according to its own established practices. But whatever system is adopted, the prime need is for it to be a recognized part of the institution's formal academic procedures. Only then can academic staff discharge their proper responsibility.

If institutions are to reap the full benefit of increased student enrollments which can follow, then above all they need to make provision for part-time study. Here too what may begin with considering administration and timetabling can quickly move into academic questions of curriculum content and design. There is only one way to make part-time study available without altering the organization of existing courses, and that is simply to permit part-time students to attend the full-time courses. This limits those who can use the facilities to those who can arrange their own lives around an institution's academic timetable. There may be variations from region to region – for instance more women than men students, though shifts in employment and retirement age mean increased numbers of men may be glad to use these opportunities for academic study – but it could produce a significant response in enrollments.

Apart from that, part-time study requires specially designed courses. They need to be arranged to allow for periodic study with credit accumulation. If they are not, then part-time study remains tied to the notion of a compulsory period of continuous study leaving individual students with as little control over their study time as full-time students except that they will be studying over a longer period and less intensively. Whilst that would be at least some extension of present provisions, if adopted generally by institutions offering full-time degrees, it would be of slight attraction to many of the kinds of students who literally cannot or do not feel able to commit themselves to four or five years of continuous study at the outset. Part-time study has to be seen as a method of enabling individuals to pursue their studies, according to their personal circumstances. Courses need to be designed as self-contained units which can also be fitted into a timetable to create a programme of study that will satisfy the academic criteria for a degree.

The basic question is the size of a self-contained unit: if it is too small the danger is of superficial study; over large and the study can be too demanding for part-time students. The best is probably a weekly commitment of about one third to one quarter of what a full-time student would undertake in the same week. A very determined and dedicated student could then study two courses simultaneously for some, if not all, of the period of part-time study, and for most it would be sufficiently demanding to require real effort, without being unduly burdensome.

One of the reasons for choosing that size is that it is about the same as many courses taught to full-time students. There are so many options within degree courses now that subjects have to be presented in relatively short periods compared to the long concentrated study typical of single or combined honours courses. Many academic staff in polytechnics and colleges are therefore already familiar with shaping their courses in this way and doing so within the academic requirements of their particular discipline and of internal credit systems. This is the central issue for specially designed courses to fit into part-time provision: that the integrity of the study is ensured. Broadly, there are two ways of doing this: a course can be self-contained in the sense that the study can properly be considered to have been completed at the end of the course; or it can be a self-contained part of a hierarchical sequence of courses in that discipline which have to be started in a prescribed order. In the sciences and technological subjects it can be held essential for subjects to be studied continuously for three or four years and for several related subjects to be undertaken simultaneously, for study to develop coherence and progress towards a rounded under-standing. In the arts and social sciences some will hold it is relatively straightforward to organize the content of courses as a series of discrete studies.

Just as with the extension of the special admission procedure to take account of experiential learning, so the arranging of academic work in this way for part-time degree courses would be no more than extending what has been done piecemeal in some institutions for a long time, and has more recently been chosen by some newer institutions as the basis of their academic organization. The tripos regulations at Cambridge University enable an undergraduate to take Part I in one discipline for the first one or two years and Part II in another quite different discipline for years two and three or year three, subject to tutorial approval and availability of places (in the sciences in particular). According to the subject, each Part may be either one or two years. So a student who had studied Classics, for example, as a two-year Part I of the tripos, could switch to Social and Political Sciences for a one-year Part II as the third year of the degree requirements, and starting from scratch would be judged to have reached honours standard in four social science options within that single year. The academic organization of Oxford Polytechnic, and the City University, is based on a matrix of all subjects so that there are a very large number of academic pathways for students to follow. Regulations restrict the range of choice a student can exercise in studying different subjects according to the requirements of each discipline. But in each case courses culminate in an examination, the results of which go towards the eventual assessment for the award of a degree.

In principle, therefore, there would seem to be no academic

objection to arranging study in courses fitted into institutional academic programmes which were organized to take full account of the varying patterns of study requested by part-time students. The practices are well established which would facilitate these developments and take full account of the standards of study required for a first degree. In principle, too, it seems perfectly possible for students to pursue their studies through a mixture of full-time and part-time study. If courses are designed as self-contained units it would not matter from an academic point of view. Again, this would simply be an extension of present practices introducing another range of possibilities for potential students.

What would be a departure from present practices is any general provision for periodic study; the facility for suspending all studies for a time, if a student wished. Except at the Open University it is not generally available to students, for institutions have no policy for allowing for credit accumulation on the basis of satisfactory performance in courses completed. In exceptional circumstances arrangements can be made for students. One who is unable to continue through illness, or change of employment, or some personal reason, may be permitted to intercalate studies by withdrawing for a year, or even – though rarely – for two. But this interruption of studies is entirely in the gift of the institution. No student can exercise it at will.

Periodic study, however, means just the opposite. As with part-time study in general, periodic study may be appropriate as a mode of working for some subjects and not for others. There might also be concern that as a result of the interruption of studies the students might not sustain their attainments. Whilst there could indeed be some danger of this, the responsibility would lie with the student to meet the required standards, rather than with the institution, and would be of no direct academic concern for the tutorial staff. It would simply be a risk incurred by the student as the price of the benefits he anticipated from being able to pause in his formal studies.

Just as for admissions, it would be open to any institution

to take steps to develop the facility for academic study. Universities can amend their statutes and ordinances for themselves on these matters. There is nothing in the proposals which requires the sanction of the Privy Council since they do not affect the original terms of a university's charter. Polytechnics and colleges teaching CNAA degrees would have to make formal submission to the Council on any topic which was considered to lie outside the terms of the approval already given. So technically there appears to be no inherent difficulty. In practice within universities or other institutions there might well be strong opposition to such proposals on all manner of grounds. That is to be expected. But for any group within an institution convinced that these developments were part of an academic policy which ought to be followed, the way is clear. The educational and financial arguments are sound. For non-university institutions there is another complication, of course. Polytechnics, colleges and institutions of education are at present constrained in making their academic developments by the course approvals system. In some cases it might be possible to develop part-time and periodic study without recourse to the full-dress approval procedure, given some skilful drafting and interpretation of present regulations. In general though, there is a serious problem and it will be explored later in this chapter.

Educational credit transfer has almost to be taken in parenthesis; it raises institutional issues of a different order. At present a student who has reasons judged to be acceptable for being unable to continue studying in one institution but could do so in another may be admitted to the second for a comparable degree course with some remission. However, rarely is any transfer to be made without loss of time – full credit transfer. Never can it be done at the sole behest of the student. As with interruption of studies, permission can only be given by institutions. On a course equivalence basis the most that can be hoped for is some regional development involving several institutions. A national system may seem only a matter for common sense arrangements; there are immense and equally commonsensical reasons why it cannot easily take place as was demonstrated by the Credit Transfer Project mentioned earlier.

There is, however, another way of considering credit transfer. Instead of looking for equivalence between the courses offered in different institutions, assessing the match between different syllabuses, it is possible to think of assessing individual students' attainment levels. As with the assessment of experiential learning as a way of matriculating candidates without formal qualifications, giving credit transfer applicants the opportunity to substantiate their claims might go some way towards producing an answer to this very vexed issue. For vexed it is. Despite, indeed perhaps because of, the wide use of credit transfer in the USA, many American academics deplore it. It is conducted by using transcripts which simply record courses taken with their results. Inevitably, given the wide variation in standards and content of courses even with the same name, and the large numbers of students in so many institutions, transcripts are sent from one registrar to another often as a purely administrative matter. That way of handling academic transfer would be unworkable for Britain, and yet some means needs to be found of enabling students particularly part-timers, to continue their studies without loss of time if they have to move from one part of the country to another. The procedures for the assessment of experiential learning could be adapted for this purpose.

Institutions have all these ways open to them of extending admission and developing opportunities for study to take account of the lives and work of candidates who may or may not have the formal qualifications, as judged at present, for eligibility for higher education. The success of these developments hinges on the attitudes of academic staff. Even if these facilities are developed, it is unlikely that recruitment would be notably successful unless the same deliberate attention is paid to teaching methods. There is always a risk among academics that though paying great attention to the content of courses, they give insufficient consideration to the way students can most effectively study the courses. That means giving the same

deliberate attention to their own teaching methods, in relation
to the particular characteristics of the students they hope to
attract as is given to courses. This is a complex problem.[1] Every
institution has a significant number of students who are capable
of so much more than they ever achieve in their academic work.
Ask any tutor. It may be the styles of teaching do not suit them,
or that they feel misunderstood by their teachers, even under-
valued, or that they find difficulty in adjusting to the ways of the
institution, or even that they are following the wrong courses
and do not have sufficient confidence in approaching any tutor
to make a change. Whatever the reason, when this happens
both student and institution are impoverished. And whatever
its appearances it is likely to be because the student and
teachers have not found ways of combining for learning. For
part-time students this difficulty can be more serious and also
less evident; more serious because the personal consequences
for an older student of experiencing any sense of failure can be
devastating, in further study which has been undertaken after
careful personal deliberation and preparation; less evident
because it is so easy for a part-time student simply to withdraw
from the course and disappear. Logically, the way to come to
terms with any problems students may experience in learning is
to begin course planning with the characteristics of the students
in mind as well as the content, so as to plot the most appropriate
routes forward to mastery of the content. For many experienced
academic teachers this may seem like putting things the wrong
way around; content is something to be mastered; there are
accepted conventions of studying to achieve that mastery; inability to work within those conventions means an inability to
study at the requisite level. For them, methodology is concerned with students finding adequate ways of studying rather

[1] Arthur W. Chickering and Associates, *The Modern American College –
Responding to the Clear Realities of Diverse Students and a Changing Society*, San
Francisco: Jossey-Bass, 1981. See also A. W. Chickering in M. T. Keeton and
Associates, *Experiential Learning: Rationale, Characteristics and Assessment*, San
Francisco: Jossey-Bass, 1977.

than the teacher's professional responsibility. The responsibility for learning is therefore the student's.

Every extension of higher education considered in this book is based on the contrary belief; that institutions should accept the responsibility for actively promoting the learning of students through every means at their disposal. That does not mean accepting responsibility for a student's learning. Quite the opposite; students must be enabled to take that responsibility for themselves, but the larger part of the enabling is the institution's essential service. There are many ways of encouraging people to learn and this is why the reconsideration of the teaching role assumes such great importance and why there is a need for some re-training of academic staff who are to work with different kinds of students.

A fundamental principle of this book is that learning should be given formal academic recognition if it is sought, irrespective of its source or how it was acquired, provided that it conforms to acceptable criteria. Thus, instead of being providers of knowledge, and making the decisions about what shall be studied and how, for some of its teaching and academic work an institution becomes a knowledge broker. It determines what the student already knows, negotiates what he wishes to study, decides appropriate forms of academic support so that he can attain the academic objectives which the institution has agreed with him are a valid course of study, puts the two together and agrees the contract for learning. This has implications for the composition of a degree study programme: it introduces the possibility of including learning derived from different sources. And it all rests on the acceptance of the principle that learning may be academically valid whatever its source always with the proviso that the recognition is an academic responsibility which can only be undertaken by academic institutions. This validation of knowledge preserves the academic integrity of the higher education system.

Institutionally and for academics this means that, through recognizing that knowledge can be generated in many different ways, they would be faithful to their own traditions of scholarship – that there are many ways of learning and none is inherently superior to others as a matter of general practice, since what matters is the level of understanding reached in any inquiry. That principle can be applied to institutions as well as to individuals. As has been shown, in America corporations such as Rank Xerox are licensed to award doctorates because of the level of teaching they provide for their own employees in order to develop their commercial interests. No such arrangement exists (yet) in Britain, and given the different organization of higher education it seems unlikely. But many industrial and multinational concerns based in Britain, such as Rolls Royce, ICI and Unilever, and in the oil industry, have advanced research establishments which rival, if not outstrip, the research facilities in some universities and polytechnics, both in staff expertise and in laboratory equipment. The increasing tendency for research contracts to be concluded between universities and industry and commerce to some extent demonstrates this, even if it has caused great controversy about the effects on the independence of universities as places of pure research. But just as these contracts point to the interdependence of higher education and industry, so too they highlight the educational implications.

Large numbers of highly qualified and widely experienced men and women who work outside formal educational institutions today are nonetheless practising as teachers. Many of the people who never think of higher education for themselves are taught by these fellow employees. At present, for most of those people, the two educational systems remain apart, which, by any token, seems very wasteful. Many follow these alternative routes towards greater knowledge and more highly developed skills; they have another source of learning but might turn to higher education to pursue their studies, if the advantages of remission were available. But if they are to have any such benefit from their life and work experience, the initiative will have to come from higher education. Perhaps one of the most convincing ways open to universities, polytechnics and colleges of demonstrating their potential value to those large sections of the population which at present tend to spurn the formal education system, once they have finished with it aged about 16 or 17, would be to be seen to be working together with employers as academic partners. They could develop an active programme of first degree courses which were jointly planned and taught. Courses could be taught in both places, or based entirely in the employer's premises if the facilities made that desirable and the content of the course made it appropriate. Others could be taught in the educational institution. Independent studies could be planned and negotiated between the student and the teacher (both employees of the same firm) and members of the institution's academic staff.

This approach underlies the sandwich course, available in some institutions, and is found within some courses for Master's degrees. There is no reason why it should not be developed for other kinds of degree courses – always with the proviso that the responsibility for the academic work remained with the institution. It would serve as a continual demonstration that higher education could be a part of the world employees inhabited. As a communication system and public relations and recruiting agency it would be very effective.

This is not the end of the matter for an institution trying to extend its academic work to appeal to wider sections of the population. Other forms of systematic preparation need to be undertaken as well: requiring a shift in the internal deployment of institutional resources. The implications for academic staff are considerable. Time spent on making independent assessments for admission, in negotiating and supervising independent studies, and in examining 'challenge course' candidates cannot be taken as minor additions to present major academic responsibilities. Part-time students mean evening teaching. This is already more highly developed in the public sector than in universities, though each institution will have some provision for evening work. But the development of part-time work of the order being suggested here implies a general acceptance by many academic staff that some regular evening teaching forms as normal a part of their work as morning or afternoon lectures. There is no other way to support a major extension of provision.

There are two other spheres of institutional activity where significant shifts would need to be made for proper academic provision of part-time study and experiential learning; administration and academic counselling. The administrative work of any Registry increases considerably with the introduction of part-time study. There is the absolute increase in the number of students' records which have to be housed, with the resultant increase in the numbers of records which have to be kept up to date at regular times during the academic year, and in the number of office staff hours occupied. The flow of information between academic staff and administration naturally increases. Computerized records can counterbalance this, but may not necessarily reduce the overall cost of record-keeping. Inevitably, too, the number of student inquiries involving administrative staff increases. Office hours may have to be extended to cope with evening attendance by part-time students who want to transact administrative business when they come to the institution for their classes. So this additional load needs proper budgetary provision if administration is to do its job of facilitating the teaching and learning of the institution.

Academic counselling runs along the border zone between academic teaching and administration. Any student needs a good deal of help in finding his way through an academic provision which offers a considerable degree of choice. Part-time students need just as much, if not more, especially if they are older students for whom the decision to study is highly significant, taken with careful deliberation. So much depends on what they now achieve; they can easily need considerable reassurance and support as well as positive guidance about the development of their programme of studies. If the intention of introducing part-time study is to attract some of the newer constituents of students, then the need for a reliable and readily available academic counselling service becomes paramount. This is not merely because of the need for support, encouragement and guidance for students who are already following courses. It is that reaching out to potential students could well be the larger part of the responsibilities of the counselling service.

An institution seeking to encourage a wider range of participants from across the socio-economic groups will need to present itself and what it can offer in terms which are readily perceived by potential students as appropriate. It is unlikely to do that unless it breaks away from the general pattern of assumptions concerning recruitment, that applicants will come to the institution to make their inquiries. As has already been made plain, for many at present who do not use higher education making direct inquiries is far too daunting for them even to consider. An academic counselling service which is going to take part-time study seriously as a prime institutional responsibility will need to be inventive in taking its wares to the people through whatever means seem appropriate in any locality. This can never be cheap, requiring highly skilled staff and information produced efficiently and imaginatively. The television age has taught people to expect professionalism in all forms of communication.

So the price of institutional development is not light. At a time of relative restriction in resources, trying to find funds for one kind of development inevitably means removing funds from some current activity, even when all the economies have been made and everything else is concentrated on essentials. The hard truth is that developing counselling and administration to support attempts to recruit different kinds of students through additional forms of study is likely to mean diverting existing resources from some current academic work. The experience of the most successful college studied in the Student Choice project referred to in Chapter 5 makes this clear. So just as some potential students may be daunted at the prospect of trying to find their way into an academic institution, so some of the academics and administrators within the institution may be

daunted at the prospect of coming to terms with the implications of trying to attract some of these potential students. But
the dividends are also potentially high; in students numbers, in
the maintenance of the higher education system. More
important, the development of higher education as an extended
service could perhaps bring a new sense of purpose, because it
was deliberately intended to meet the circumstances of its age.

This preparation will be pointless, indeed it is highly unlikely
to be undertaken at all unless government recognizes that it has
a vital part to play and is prepared to play it for non-university
institutions. There are two matters of policy which it alone can
decide: the financing of part-time study; and the system of
approving courses. Both of these matters apply directly to polytechnics and colleges and institutes of higher education because
as public sector institutions they are directly controlled by
government systems of finance and administration. The first
policy area could have considerable significance for universities
as well, making some impact on financial calculations made by
the University Grants Committee in its negotiations with the
DES and the Treasury.

The personal financing of part-time students through
maintenance grants has been discussed already. For institutions there is a different issue. They need to be sure that there is
no risk of part-time provision being attempted on the cheap.
The finance for part-time degree courses needs to be proportionately on the same basis as for full-time students. That is not
quite so straightforward as it might seem. Each half-time student is more expensive for an institution to teach than half a
full-time student, in terms of administration, teaching, library
and catering costs. The budget for part-time provision would
need to be based on a realistic calculation of this disproportion-
ate expense. Otherwise the additional resources could only be
found by raiding the finance for full-time students; hardly an
acceptable way to make an unofficial policy decision. So government action is essential. This does not necessarily mean an
absolute increase in expenditure; that is a different matter. It

concerns the basis on which calculations are made for financing part-time degree courses. If the calculations are equitable, institutions will be better able to make suitable distributions to support full-time and part-time study, within whatever funds are made available.

The problem with the course approval system is that it is mixed up with overriding government statutory responsibilities for controlling expenditure. Government control of courses gives it control over numbers of students and staff, and so over money. It is a highly complex question,[1] but the solution is to reach some rational division between the financial control and academic development. At present polytechnics and colleges are hedged around with a labyrinth of requirements before any degree level course can be offered. This makes it extremely difficult, if not impossible, for an institution to plan its academic provision on any rational basis. They submit proposals for degree courses to the Regional Advisory Committee (RAC) knowing that the DES can veto any recommendation made by that Committee through the Regional Staff Inspector who has to approve all courses before they can be taught. They submit financial estimates to the local authority (or in the case of voluntary colleges, to the DES direct), knowing that approval is linked to approval of the course by the RAC and DES. They can then find, as they frequently do, that the approval itself is linked to academic and institutional conditions which may conflict with the design and institutional context of the course in question. Frustrating as this is for administration, this byzantine procedure is highly wasteful of the very energy and imagination which are needed for the development of courses and teaching. There are other ways for government to exercise its statutory responsibility in maintaining financial control. The principle is clear. There needs to be clearer separation of financial and academic functions than at present. As the authority for use of

[1] Department of Education and Science, *Report of the Working Group on the Management of Higher Education in the Maintained Sector*, Cmnd 7130, London: HMSO, 1978 (known as the Oakes Report).

public funds, government must exercise control over financial expenditure. Institutions cannot expect to be allowed to develop as they wish with someone else footing the bill. However, institutions must have prime control over their own academic development within set financial limits. There is no other way to channel the initiative and energy of their staffs to the need for higher education to develop its services.

Appropriate changes in financing part-time courses and in the system of course approvals would enable institutions to assume their proper responsibility for developing their higher education services according to the circumstances dictated by their geographical area. For public sector institutions, however, there would be one huge additional benefit: the saving of time and money facilitated by a speedier response. At present it takes about three years between designing a course and teaching the first students, so complex and protracted are the various procedures. This is obviously frustrating and can be discouraging for the staff, given the uncertainties at every stage with the continual risks of wasted effort. But in working for a better match between what institutions offer and what individuals may wish to study, there is a far more serious risk – of wasted opportunities. Changes in economic and social conditions with complex interactions in employment do not occur at such a leisurely pace. Institutions need to be able to respond far more quickly than that if they are to move towards providing the courses that people actually want. So change in government policy is part of the necessary preparation to enable higher education to get on with its job.

The whole of this chapter depends on the assumption that whether the academic work comes from part-time study, or from any inclusion of experiential learning, the attainment levels of the students will emulate those expected of full-time students in similar studies. This raises the complex question of the standards required for the award of a first degree. There is no rubric which defines it, nor could there be. The content of courses is always changing, the balance between breadth of study and depth of study is always being adjusted, and most usually is a subject of dispute. New 'subjects' appear; new combinations of study areas are produced; the length of courses varies. In some universities four courses taken in a year are deemed to reach a standard which is appropriate for a fully classified honours degree. In other institutions an arithmetic sum of the results of courses taken over three years enables a student to be awarded an Ordinary or Honours degree. It is not possible to compare the standards required for degrees of the same class between different disciplines, despite continual insistence on the need for the most rigorous policing of the standards of a first degree.

External examiners are the safeguards of these standards. By holding an academic appointment in one institution and examining in another, there is a continual interchange of information and critical discussion about the study in each discipline taught in every institution in Britain which offers first degrees. The academic community appoints from its own numbers, and sometimes from experts in the field not holding formal academic appointments, a kind of priesthood charged with the task of ensuring the purity of academic work. When buttressed with all the examination boards that consider students' results before an award is made, on the whole it is a system which seems to work reasonably well. Certainly no better arrangement has yet been invented. But it all goes no further than supporting the staff of the institutions in their own tasks of making academic judgements about attainment levels as part of their daily job. So while there are no rubrics about standards, there is a fairly well understood and accepted understanding of what those standards are.

The assessment of experiential learning can thus be contained within this system of academic quality control. Whatever the problems of making reliable and valid assessments of the knowledge and skills derived from non-classroom activities, either within or beyond the influence of academic staff, there are understood standards which have to be observed. This offers a source of security. Judgements of attainment levels derived from experiential learning would have to be submitted to the various academic committees before they are finally accepted. This is where precision and clarity become so important. It is the easiest thing in the world to be deluded about standards because of the way the assessment system works. Reliable and valid assessment depends on a coincidence between what is to be learned and what is assessed. The task, therefore, in assessing experiential learning is to produce a set of results which is no less reliable than those submitted for conventionally taught courses.

It is one thing to talk about the maintenance of academic standards; it is quite another to take full account of the kinds of unfamiliar demands which are made on academic staff by the developments proposed in this chapter. Yet, if the institutions are to offer their services to wider sections of the population than they appeal to at present, experiential learning has to be taken into academic consideration – that is knowledge and skills have a recognizable existence whether they are the result of formal tuition or not, and as such demand due academic recognition. To talk of institutions is merely to talk of the people who make them up, and so it is the staffs of academic institutions who have to be convinced. Beleaguered as they are with reductions of expenditure and threats of greater reductions still, it may seem untimely to expect hard-pressed men and women to undertake academic roles which may appear foreign. Yet extensions of the present provision and, especially, serious investigation of the possibilities of experiential learning offer a way of breaking out of the siege into the open country. No new development of any kind will be possible unless the staffs accept them. Staff will only find them acceptable through careful consideration of what is involved.

Reductions in student numbers will affect institutions unevenly. For those who may begin to worry about their recruitment, deliberate preparation for developing their provision for additional and new constituents of students seems essential. For those who worry about educational provision, the changes outlined in the last two chapters can offer some opportunities for development to reverse the dismaying recession of the moment. The opportunities may not be at all what academic staff anticipated when they began their careers; but they exist. Some new sense of purpose could come from pursuing them and could lift the low morale induced by the present static, if not retrogressive, conditions. There could even be some comfort in reflecting that this kind of redirection during mid-career is now affecting education as it has long since affected many occupations. Education has been seen as standing aloof from the day to day business of making the money which finances it. Now it is being sucked into the consequence of the workaday world not making enough money, and doesn't like it; not unnaturally. But as for any other enterprise, there are some positive responses possible, if there is the will to make them.

7

Conclusions

Higher education has always been a powerful force for change; in some ages strongly influenced by research. As new discoveries or new interpretations work their ways into the bloodstream of national life, social and political structures alter over time. The mid-nineteenth-century Darwinian debates between scientists and theologians on the nature of man give a vivid example. We live with the results of Keynesian economics as yet unresolved. At other times, however, institutional changes in higher education have a more obvious direct influence on society. Again, taking another example from the nineteenth century, there was the opening of Oxford and Cambridge universities to non-conformists and Roman Catholics. Until the University Tests Act of 1871 'the ancient universities of Oxford and Cambridge were still virtually closed to dissenters and Roman Catholics by religious tests.'[1] The Robbins Report is a more recent example; as a force for change it is unmistakable. At present higher education potential as an institutional force for change is just as great as in the post-Robbins years, if not greater. And its services are needed.

It can offer services to adults they cannot obtain elsewhere and which increasing numbers are likely to want. It is becoming more important every day in more types of employment to have the best possible qualifications, to be capable of benefiting from

[1] R. C. K. Ensor, *England 1870–1914*, The Oxford History of England vol. XIV, London: OUP, 1936.

appropriate re-training, and to have opportunities for keeping up to date through taking post-experience courses. It is becoming increasingly important, too, for many to enhance their own view of their status by becoming better qualified, and to have the pleasures which come from studying at a level which brings deep personal satisfaction. For many adults the needs are clear. Higher education can go to meet them, if it chooses. The complement to this is that higher education services are equally needed by employers whether in industry, or in commerce, or in corporations, all the institutions of government and the professions.

Nowadays the success of any enterprise depends on everyone being as knowledgeable as possible in their particular field of work. At both corporate and individual levels therefore the services higher education can offer make it a potent force for change. There is one other unique service which higher education can provide, and this is for the traditional eighteen-plus students. Within an academic study for a degree, it can offer opportunities for personal growth and development as part of career education. As employment becomes more difficult to obtain, young people are increasingly at a loss without this rounded preparation. Here again the significance of higher education's contribution is clear.

Correspondingly it is vital for higher education institutions to realise their own potential. If they do not, research itself is likely to suffer, bringing an overall impoverishment of the nation's intellectual life and incalculable economic and social consequences. For whatever special research funds are made available from public and private purses it is the size of student recruitment to institutions which creates the essential base for research capacity. But higher education can only achieve this if it becomes far more responsive than it is at present to individuals and to other institutions in society.

The most critical question about higher education is how much do we need? The answer should by now be clear; as much as people want (which depends on what is offered) and can be paid for. Manpower planning; cost effectiveness in relation to subsequent national economic benefits; defining the size of the pool of ability from which students come; all are now known to be far too approximate to produce reliable answers. No one can predict the consequences on higher education application rates of the dramatic changes in employment arising from the combination of worldwide economic problems and the invention of the microprocessor. Age participation, opportunity and eligibility rates based on past experience may be the best guide there is and may turn out to be reasonably accurate, but cannot be relied on with much confidence. As with withdrawal rates, comparisons are misleading. But it is worth noting that opinion in Australia, the USA and Britain is that the age participation rates are likely to decline. The steady state has gone, perhaps forever, in education as in everything else. So the answer to the question of how much education we need can only be given ultimately through counting up the places which are filled. Places will only be filled if higher education itself accepts that it too must change in its view of individuals and of its relation with other institutions their present circumstances.

Perhaps the most important of these changed circumstances is the alteration in psychologists' understanding of individuals. Any educationalist knows the world is full of late developers. Psychologists, from their recent studies of adult human development, now recognise that there are successive phases as well as ages and stages through which each person passes and that each poses its own particular requirements for new learning to achieve the most satisfying life in each period. Each period therefore offers fresh opportunities and, for many, new needs to study to acquire new learning. They say, further, that there is no precise correlation between chronological age and developmental stage. Each person's most effective way of learning at any time is therefore influenced by the combination of both. In general that raises curriculum and methodological issues for higher education's approach to traditional 18 plus students now. Any introduction of considerable numbers of older adults to higher education raises these issues in acute and specific terms.

This becomes evident when the changes in understanding of human growth and development are set alongside the institutional changes now affecting increasing numbers; their families, employment and leisure, and provision for ageing and dying. These interlocking experiences can all be related to further study. Opportunities appeal to different people differently, and for different reasons because of their different circumstances, but each opportunity taken, whether for career or for personal development, influences work, family, leisure and all.

This book's proposals for extending higher education provision are all made on the basis that due recognition must be given to knowledge and skills acquired by individuals whatever their source and whenever they may have been acquired. Institutions must accept responsibility for making academic judgements about attainment levels in knowledge and skills that they had no direct part in transmitting. It also means them accepting a similar responsibility for students' knowledge and skills acquired through practical experience organised under an institution's authority as part of a degree. Academic institutions must be prepared to extend their validation and accrediting roles. Instead of confining their judgements to what is learned from courses provided as their institution's formal responsibility, academic staff need to be making judgements about the levels of learning reached through a variety of other means. It makes no difference whether the candidate for this form of judgement learned from reading, evening classes, study groups, daily employment, following Open University programmes for fun or from the television or radio. Two things matter: that the possibility is acknowledged that significant intellectual activity leading to the acquisition of knowledge and skills can take place without interference from formal educational institutions; that assessment of the breadth and depth of knowledge acquired is made by an acknowledged academic authority. Knowledge needs to be recognised wherever it is found.

The acceptance of this extended academic responsibility would alter substantially the relationship between individuals as learners and institutions as resources for learning. Instead of being constrained within the boundaries of the formal organisation of learning, intending learners will be free to act as independent agents, working where they choose and accepting responsibility for the results of their work. Many, probably most, students will continue to want the security given by formal taught courses for substantial portions of their studies. But the decision should be theirs. This is the reality of the different relationship between academic institutions and individuals which this enlargement of higher education involves.

Such developments would be the most significant indication that higher education is responding to society. It would demonstrate that it accepted as partners any other sources of learning leading to academic attainment. If institutions combined these approaches with administrative measures to enable more people to attend courses then the message of welcome to potential students would be unmistakeable. It would become stronger still if institutions offered combinations of full-time and part-time study instead of just one or the other, with opportunities for taking a complete break from study. There can be little doubt that these possible permutations of study would be a great attraction.

Any alteration in the relationship between potential students and institutions means shifts in another crucial relationship: the academic world and the world of work. For a large number, if not a majority, of those who might want part-time study, it is their employer who determines the study pattern. If the habit of part-time study is developed, even without any form of paid educational leave[1], trade unions' negotiations with employers

---

[1] For discussion see Colin Fletcher in *Higher Education for All?* edited by Gordon W. Roderick and Michael Stephens, Brighton: The Falmer Press, 1980. See also *Education and Work: A Study of Paid Educational Leave in England and Wales 1976/77* by John Killeen and Margaret Bird, Leicester: National Institute for Adult Education, 1981.

would soon include facilities for study which would benefit their members without damaging the employer, and that would bring into negotiations the college, polytechnic or university concerned. In any such negotiations the role of the institutions of higher education is crucial, and that role is best approached through considering the relationship between trade unions and higher education. So far little has been said about trade unions' significance for higher education. However, they are every bit as important as employers. The demographic, technological, economic, cultural and political changes in British society are challenging the traditions of trade unions as they are higher education.

So is the knowledge explosion which is revolutionizing the nature of work. It is altering the overall composition of trade union membership with increasing proportions of white rather than blue collar workers, and so giving increasing emphasis to overall conditions of service in negotiations between unions and employers.

Emphasis on shorter working hours, conditions of early retirement, and holiday entitlements are adding complexities to any wage and salary negotiations. At the same time employment legislation requires trade union officials to be increasingly knowledgeable about the law and to develop sophisticated skills in interpreting it. The potential benefits from higher education are considerable for individual members and for trade unions as institutions.

However, before potential benefit can become actual benefit, higher education has to demonstrate a far greater willingness to work with employers and trade unions than it has so far. At present neither automatically thinks of turning to higher education as the most likely partner for the further education of their members and employees. (The same is true for many men and women who did not turn to higher education when they were younger. They do not automatically think of trying to find out what use it might be to them.) It is up to the institutions to take the initiative in trying to change all that.

The case is that experiential learning can offer a new beginning. This is the Knowledge Revolution, making the link between learning and work. If knowledge is knowledge wherever it is found became a watchword for action and not a catch phrase for rhetoric, a great deal of the hostility which can mar the exchanges between employers and educators might be reduced. When an employer realised that what an employee had learned through his work either had gained academic recognition or was a base for further study that could gain academic recognition, his view of higher education could change. Similarly, when trade unionists realised that the experience of officials and members could be the source of recognised academic learning their conceptions of higher education institutions and what they had to offer could change. In our society recognition of this kind counts for much. Some would go as far as to say that the lack of it at present and the resulting lack of mutual confidence between employers and educators is the most important factor in explaining the reluctance of able young graduates and school-leavers to enter the production services instead of the professions. Institutions of higher education could go a long way to change this by extending their validation to include the knowledge and skills acquired at work.

It would be a mistake to give the impression that no such co-operation exists at present. It does indeed. Unfortunately, however, there is still insufficient co-operation. Government, employer, trade union, and institute of higher education, each one continues to complain about the lack of sufficient collaboration without much effect. With so many calls for action, and such acute economic and political problems, national and international, now would seem a particularly good time for something to be done.

Much can happen with experiential learning as a common denominator between the world of work and higher education. Bilateral negotiations can take place between higher education and employers or trade unions at local or national levels. Better still trilateral explorations could be undertaken. Discussions should include not only appropriate content of courses but the entire context in which opportunities for learning are offered. The question 'Where?' is as important as the question 'How?' A course offered in a factory or corporation or trade union branch building says as much and perhaps more about co-operation and partnership than the most carefully negotiated programme of courses. A course will be disastrous if it is taught by a teacher who is discomforted at finding himself tested for his academic credentials by students who are experienced trade unionists accustomed to testing managers in tough negotiations. It is clear that if higher education is to provide appropriate services for those working in industry and commerce it has to accept the full implications of partnership. Whilst retaining its proper academic responsibility for determining ultimately what counts as appropriate knowledge for the award of a degree, it has to accept that much, perhaps even most, of the content needs to be negotiated rather than prescribed. Both trade unions and employers have essential responsibilities towards their own people in seeing that courses of study are appropriate. Collaboration can only be successful if those responsibilities are given due weight in academic decisions which affect them directly.

Some further examples from the United States are instructive. Since 1973 Wayne State University in Detroit has run a Weekend College Programme intended to serve working class adults. Currently there are 1200 students. The teaching is through a combination of television presentations, workshop seminars and intensive weekend conferences. Television programmes are shown at various times during the week. Workshop sessions are held weekly in church halls, union halls, high schools and municipal libraries, as well as in the university, at different times so that most students can attend conveniently near either home or work. There are eight weekend conferences during the year on the university campus. For the first two years students follow three courses, one from each of the divisions of humanities, social science and technology. The courses are organized round a common theme of the lives of working adults, covering subjects such as the nature of work and the work force with emphasis on the nature and structure of labour institutions. In the third and fourth years theory and method courses which examine the assumptions and methodologies of and the connections between the humanities, social science, and technology, take most of the time, with the rest being given to a long essay on a topic of particular interest. It might be a study of a period of literature, the development of black Detroit, grievance procedure or union history.

Another Labour programme is the result of the most unlikely collaboration between District 37 (New York City) of the American Federation of State, County and Municipal Employees and a small Catholic Liberal Arts college for women: La Rochelle. The DC 37 Campus is governed, staffed and funded jointly by union and college. Extensive use is made of the assessment of experiential learning along the lines shown in Chapter 4. There are seven hundred students, of whom some four hundred and fifty, mainly women in clerical jobs, attend in the evening, nearly two hundred are retired union members and about one hundred family service paraprofessionals, also predemoninantly women attend mainly in the afternoons. The curriculum is largely interdisciplinary, tackling topics such as the Urban Community, the Human Body, Science and Human Values, the American Experience and the American Trade Union Movement. The underlying assumption of the entire programme is that adults learn best when they accept considerable responsibility for deciding their own learning goals.

Empire State College of the State University of New York has its own Labour College in New York City, offering a curriculum which combines labour orientated liberal arts courses with specialized labour studies courses. Its success makes it confident that it will be able to offer the same specialized academic service, including research, to the labour movement that professional education offers to industry business and agriculture at college level. In each of these cases the higher education institution took the initiative and approached the trade unions. On the basis of a wary recognition of common interests, though perhaps with different origins, a highly productive collaboration has grown with clear gain for each partner.

In theory, similar opportunities are available to institutions in Britain, to develop special relationships with special interest groups producing special courses for special purposes. Ruskin College, Oxford, and Middlesex and Leicester Polytechnics are just some examples of what can be done. But present academic procedures make for difficulties in relating these courses to degree work directly. In practice, money makes things particularly difficult, and more will be said about that a little later. More significant, though, is the view of most trade unionists that higher education is not capable of providing them with any service which they would value. It is not quite so bad with employers, but that may be because they tend to think of higher education in relation to management recruitment, rather than to skilled workers and union activists.

The University of Aston has developed successfully Master's degrees which are to some extent a shared responsibility between university and industry. There has also been a fairly substantial increase in short post-experience courses as a result of collaboration between higher education and employers. But essentially the same point obtains. If higher education wants to extend its recruitment into adults at work, then it has to make positive moves towards employers and trade unions to convince them that collaboration is worthwhile.[1]

However successful the collaboration between higher education, employers and trade unions might be, unfortunately it is the case that nothing worthwhile is likely to develop at all unless something is done about the most intractable problems for higher education as it tries to innovate – money. It is not part of the thesis of this book that more money should be made

[1] For information on what is available at present see M. Locke and J. Pratt, *A Guide to Learning After School*, Harmondsworth: Penguin, 1979; A. Pates and M. Good, *Second Chances for Adults: Your Guide to All Kinds of Education and Training Opportunities*, London: Macmillan, 1980.

available. Whatever can be done to attune higher education more closely to the society which supports it must be done within existing financial limits. At the most optimistic, sufficient money may be made available to preserve the present framework and most of the institutions. At worst, pressure from taxpayers, as well as governments of any complexion trying to cope with inflation and a drooping economy, and reductions in expenditure, will push education so far down the order of priorities as public spending on hospitals, social services, and housing are seen to offer more immediate benefits, that the post-Robbins world of higher education will be destroyed, so that opportunities will actually diminish. Improved relationships with employers and trade unions is therefore crucial for higher education, as part of a general strategy for trying to preserve its financial and institutional position.

But even if the best occurs, it will be extremely difficult for any coherent developments to take place along the lines of part-time study and curriculum development based on experiential learning unless significant changes are made to the overall deployment of the money expended on student grants. Two problems need to be solved. One is the financial support for part-time students, the other is giving the power to men and women to study when they choose. With the present accent on re-training, redeployment and redundancy, it is impossible to justify simultaneously the automatic entitlement to maintenance grants for 18 to 21 or 22 year old full-time students, even with the parental means test at present in force, and the denial of such entitlement to older part-time students which leaves them at the arbitrary mercy of a local education authority's policy over discretionary grants: 'Just under half the authorities are showing a decrease in expenditure on discretionary grants . . .'[1] If the present total expenditure on student grants is maintained, and the numbers of full-time students falls, in

[1] Department of Education and Science, *Report by Her Majesty's Inspectorate on the Effects on the Education Service of England and Wales of Local Authority Expenditure Polices – 1980/1981*, HMSO, 1981.

theory there might be some possibility of using whatever money was left over for grants for part-time students. In practice such a neat balancing act is highly improbable, and in any case does not really face the problem squarely.

Perhaps the best way of bringing some rationality into discussions about higher education fees and student grants is to introduce full-cost fees for courses so that, whether home or overseas students are considered, the costs of higher education would be more generally understood by local and national politicians as well as the electorate. Levels of expenditure and ways of meeting them could then be discussed differently. The debate could be couched in similar terms to the financing of local authority housing (rents, rates and central subsidies) or medical and social services (national insurance payments by employers and employees, entitlements to various payments and the prescription and dental charges). If there was not enough money to finance grants for full-time students and part-time students then the available money would be redistributed between full-time students, and additional money sought. Some system of student loans, backed by government banks and finance houses for all or part of full-cost fees is one possible source. They would hardly encourage wider participation from population groups which have eschewed higher education so far, and it is the case of this book that every development envisaged should have that as an objective. The most obvious action is to award each person a post-secondary education study entitlement say on the eighteenth birthday, perhaps index linked, which could be used to pay fees and provide maintenance support for periods of full-time or part-time study at any time of the person's choosing. Once that award was used up it would be the responsibility of individuals to find financial support themselves, through their firms, loans, charities and foundations or savings. How many years of full-time study or the equivalent in part-time study each award would be worth would need careful calculation. But as a principle on which to finance student study in higher education at least it is defensible in terms of all students, unlike the present funding.

The effect of such an alteration on institutions is unpredictable. What proportion of present full-time 18-plus students would not see the full three years straight through if they knew that they could still be grant aided later after making a break in their studies, it is impossible to say. Quite a few, one would guess. Much more to the point of this book is the way this would alter the relationship between potential and actual students and institutions. Part-time study might well expand rapidly, as younger men and women decided to try and insure themselves for employment and subsequent advancement through taking on a job and part-time study simultaneously. Others might see it as a way of spreading financial payments to make best use of their award. But more important it would put a premium on an institution's ability to provide courses which would attract students; it would tend to encourage institutions to respond more readily to the conditions of potential students. It could give an incentive to potential students and institutions alike to develop the applications explored earlier in this book of experiential learning within academic programmes.

If the financing of higher education stays more or less as it is, with improved conditions for part-time students, then no major changes are likely to transform the higher education system. Neither the introduction of part-time study as a general facility, nor the inclusion of experiential learning within academic programme, would achieve that. Between them part-time study and experiential learning offer considerable opportunities for this provided they are backed up by a fundamental change in financing.

In practice, some institutions are going to change while others will not. Some will continue to enjoy healthy recruitment and see no need to change; others are likely to shrink. Part-time study and experiential learning are catalysts for effecting a change in provision in those institutions which choose to develop these facilities. (The latest position seems to be that part-time degrees are available in three universities and are under consideration in another six.) The essential point is that universities, polytechnics and colleges offer broadly similar courses and that these some 150 institutions must offer a wider range of opportunities for study than at present. This simply requires adding to existing provision in those places where it seems desirable to do so because of local circumstances.

There is one innovation, however, which would be entirely new and could be the most direct way of providing additional facilities. It is an extension of the various versions to be found of an Open College.[1] An additional institution or units within existing institutions could be established to provide agency services for external study. The story of external degrees in Britain is honourable, and, indeed, distinguished. Before they were chartered, the universities of Exeter, Hull, Nottingham and Southampton were established as university colleges authorized to teach their students as external candidates for the degree examinations of the University of London. London University itself accepted candidates for external degrees irrespective of how they had prepared themselves for the examinations. More often than not, they were supported by the various correspondence colleges, although that was a matter of their own choice. However, since 1972 it has not been possible for overseas students to register as external degree candidates. London University does continue to offer external degrees, although in a limited range of subjects.[2] This facility should be replaced by another, with wider possibilities for study.

A college of further education or a polytechnic could submit for approval by a university, or the Council for National Academic Awards, a degree programme which offered some or all of the facilities sketched in earlier chapters. A university could offer the facility itself. In theory, it would be possible for a new institution to be established for the purpose. Entrance

---

[1] See Enid and Edward Hutchinson, *Learning Later*, Routledge and Kegan Paul, 1978.

[2] B.D., B.A. in one subject, LL.B., B. Mus., B.Sc. (Econ.).

procedures would be based on judgements about competence for further study, rather than on records of previous study. They could include provision for the assessment of previously acquired learning from life and work experience. Classes could be provided in convenient localities for groups of students who wished to have their prior learning assessed in this way. In those classes they would find support and encouragement from fellow students as well as professional help in learning to organize their educational autobiographies or portfolios, so as to identify clearly what they claimed to have learned and where, and how that learning could be verified. Students would be admitted with advanced standing and remission of course if the assessments of their learning demonstrated appropriate attainment levels. Part of the work of that class or another special one would be to design individual learning programmes for completing the degree. The degree programme could be organized under the broad divisions of humanities, social sciences and science and technology, with a mixture of prescribed study and a range of supporting options studies. The specific requirements could be tested through formal examinations set for the purpose, leaving it to the responsibility of the student to choose the method of preparation. That could be through private study (even private coaching) or through attending courses offered in a nearby institution, through existing correspondence courses, following Open University courses – whichever was preferable. The supporting options could be undertaken as independent studies. Work and life experience could form a basis for further study if it was agreed in a learning programme. A second assessment of those learning experiences could be conducted to support claims to knowledge which a student felt he had mastered and had learned how to articulate during his study. Courses studied either before registration for the degree or afterwards at an appropriate level could be considered as counting towards the degree results provided they fitted into the learning agreements. The programme would provide for credit accumulation over a period of time, facilitating periodic study. The academic services could be available all the year round without fixed terms, although there might have to be set times for registration so that students could select for themselves the most convenient times to begin and complete their studies.

Such a provision would complement the work of the Open University. It could be organized locally, regionally or nationally. It would provide for those who did not wish to join the Open University and who either could not or did not wish to make use of whatever facilities were provided in their own locality. This would be in line with the general requirement of extending facilities to enable the maximum number to participate. It would be another way of recognising that people's circumstances so often prevent them from fulfilling the personal gratifications of study they desire, and of taking steps to meet them.

It might be possible for such an institution to go one step further to include sub-degree work as a preparatory stage as was discussed in Chapter 5. This could provide time and space for adults to try themselves out at further study without pressure from the fear of academic failure. It could go beyond that. 'Inquiry' classes could be arranged to provide opportunities for men and women to come to a reliable assessment of their strengths and weaknesses, their capacity for academic study and whether it was in their interests to undertake it, given their home and work circumstances.

The staffing of such a programme could be arranged, with the smallest possible number of full-time central administrative and academic staff with responsibility for the programme, and with part-time tutors employed specially to take assessment classes, teach courses which groups of students wanted where these were not already provided in institutions, act as learning programme advisers, conduct assessment of experiential learning, and formal examinations where these were required. The composition of the part-time staff would change from year to year as with Adult Education at present, according to the requirements of the student body. That could ensure that there was never more than a necessary financial commitment, at the same time as maintaining the flexibility for meeting the requirements of a changing student population.

In addition to receiving academic validation, such a scheme for an additional institution would require authorization from the Department of Education and Science, unless (as with Buckingham University College) the scheme was undertaken independently of public funds in the initial stages and sought public support subsequently. If an existing public institution wanted to undertake such a development the DES would in effect hold a veto. All of which reverts to the passage in Chapter 2 concerning the government's inescapable responsibility for enabling institutions to become more responsive. Government must reconsider its own role in the present confusion between necessary financial controls, with approval procedures for academic courses, which effectively inhibit the responsible academic development of institutions it has itself created.

Higher education's most promising future lies in extending its services to the widest range and variety of participants. Institutional responsibility is clear, and that includes the institutions of central and local government; to see that people get what they wish to use, always with the proviso that responsibility for academic standards is preserved.

What matters most to mankind is a sense of self esteem. It is the source of self confidence which accepts personal strengths and weaknesses and sustains a sense of well being within which other things that matter most can take their proper place – the love and friendship of others, the pleasure of creative activities or the appreciation of the creative powers of others in writing art, music, films and theatre. It is here that education is so crucial.

The high hopes of the 1944 Education Act have so largely been disappointed that, for all the effort put into trying to improve the system of schools and higher education,[1] and

---

[1] See Shirley Williams, *Politics is for People*, Harmondsworth: Penguin, 1981.

making personal growth and development through learning more possible for more people, the net result has been to produce a society which in many ways feels it has been sold short. Instead of giving encouragement to those who need it most, the system passes them by and even discourages them. This is not in the least the intention; yet it is what happens all too often. The reason is that we have not shown enough understanding or curiosity about the way pupils and potential students receive what institutions offer them. Quite simply we have not respected them enough for what they are and what they might become. Equality of opportunity can never be realised without that respect. The assessment of experiential learning, with all the curriculum implications which follow, is based on respect for what people know however they may have learned it. It enables a person to reveal what he knows instead of making assumptions about what he needs to reveal in order to be recognized as fit for further study. In some ways, therefore, recognition of experiential learning can offer a fresh start for the educational policy of equality of opportunity. And it does so in quite direct personal terms. This is looking for ways of enabling people to demonstrate their capabilities and so be valued for what they are.

At the beginning of this book the reader was asked to keep clearly in mind the needs and well-being of individuals as actual and potential students, whatever the discussion of complex institutional issues, and it is with the individuals that this book must end. This is what the Knowledge Revolution, making the link between learning and work, is trying to show is possible. It is not asking for more of everything in higher education. It is arguing for the systematic consideration of a few specific lines of development because they are appropriate at present. To turn them into a daily experience for men and women requires an imaginative leap by the leadership and academic staff of some universities, polytechnics and colleges, each acting within its own circumstances. The past thirty years have seen leaders and staff acting with great ingenuity in coping with the impressive expansion in numbers of students. Now we need to see the same imagination and energy used in enlarging the scope of higher education: redefining its purpose and practices for the remainder of the century to provide – in that little phrase of Robbins – for 'those who want to'.

This book has argued for a change in the present state of affairs for the large number of individuals of society who have the capacity for further study. That does not for one moment imply that by some automatic process participation in higher education will transform them. Rather, it argues that the experience of systematic study equips people to organize their lives more effectively to their own and others' satisfaction and that the more people who are so equipped the better for our technological society. They may be better able to live their own lives, less likely to have them lived for them, more able and willing to respect others' lives. This is a proper purpose for our education, especially higher education; the more of it the better.

Index